Primary Source Document Workbook

for

World Civilizations

Second Edition

Robert Welborn
Clayton State College

West
Thomson Learning.

Australia • Canada • Denmark • Japan • Mexico • New Zealand • Philippines
Puerto Rico • Singapore • South Africa • Spain • United Kingdom • United States

COPYRIGHT © 2000 Wadsworth. West is an imprint of Wadsworth, a division of Thomson Learning. Thomson Learning is a trademark used herein under license.

All Rights Reserved. No part of this work may be reproduced, transcribed, or used in any form or by any means—graphic, electronic, or mechanical, including photocopying, recording, taping, Web distribution, or information storage and retrieval systems—without the prior written permission of the publisher.

Printed in the United States of America

1 2 3 4 5 6 7 03 02 01 00 99

> For permission to use material from this text, contact us by
>   Web: www.thomsonrights.com
>   Fax: 1-800-730-2215
>   Phone: 1-800-730-2214

ISBN 0-534-56923-4

For more information, contact
Wadsworth/Thomson Learning
10 Davis Drive
Belmont, CA 94002-3098
USA
www.wadsworth.com

International Headquarters
Thomson Learning
290 Harbor Drive, 2nd Floor
Stamford, CT 06902-7477
USA

UK/Europe/Middle East
Thomson Learning
Berkshire House
168-173 High Holborn
London WC1V 7AA
United Kingdom

Asia
Thomson Learning
60 Albert Complex
Singapore 189969

Canada
Nelson/Thomson Learning
1120 Birchmount Road
Scarborough, Ontario M1K 5G4
Canada

TABLE OF CONTENTS

PREFACE..1

CHAPTER 1
PREHISTORY...2

CHAPTER 2
MESOPOTAMIA..3

CHAPTER 3
EGYPT..5

CHAPTER 4
EMPIRES AND THEOLOGY IN THE NEAR EAST................7

CHAPTER 5
INDIA'S BEGINNINGS..8

CHAPTER 6
ANCIENT CHINA TO 500 B.C.E. 10

CHAPTER 7
ORDINARY LIVES IN THE ANCIENT PAST......................12

CHAPTER 8
THE GREEK ADVENTURE..13

CHAPTER 9
HELLENIC CULTURE...15

CHAPTER 10
HELLENISTIC CIVILIZATION...17

CHAPTER 11
THE ROMAN REPUBLIC..19

CHAPTER 12
THE ROMAN EMPIRE..21

CHAPTER 13
ORDINARY LIVES IN THE CLASSICAL AGE....................22

CHAPTER 14
ROME'S TRANSFORMATION AND THE BEGINNINGS
OF EUROPE...23

CHAPTER 15
ISLAM...26

CHAPTER 16
MATURE ISLAMIC SOCIETY AND INSTITUTIONS............28

CHAPTER 17
INDIAN CIVILIZATION IN ITS GOLDEN AGE.................. 30

CHAPTER 18
CHINA TO THE MONGOL CONQUEST........................... 31

CHAPTER 19
JAPAN AND SOUTHEAST ASIA..................................... 33

CHAPTER 20
AFRICA FROM KUSH TO 1500....................................... 35

CHAPTER 21
THE AMERICAS BEFORE COLUMBUS.......................... 37

CHAPTER 22
ORDINARY LIFE AMONG THE NON-WESTERN PEOPLES.. 39

CHAPTER 23
THE HIGH MEDIEVAL AGE... 41

CHAPTER 24
LATE MEDIEVAL TROUBLES....................................... 44

CHAPTER 25
THE EUROPEAN RENAISSANCE................................... 45

CHAPTER 26
A LARGER WORLD OPENS... 47

CHAPTER 27
THE PROTESTANT REFORMATION............................... 50

CHAPTER 28
FOUNDATIONS OF THE EUROPEAN STATES................. 53

CHAPTER 29
EAST EUROPEAN EMPIRES... 55

CHAPTER 30
CHINA FROM THE MING TO THE EARLY
QING DYNASTY.. 57

CHAPTER 31
JAPAN AND COLONIAL SOUTHEAST ASIA
TO THE NINETEENTH CENTURY.................................. 59

CHAPTER 32
THE RISE AND FALL OF THE MUSLIM EMPIRES............. 61

CHAPTER 33
AFRICA: FROM COMMERCIAL PARTNER TO COLONY... 63

CHAPTER 34
LATIN AMERICA FROM COLONY TO DEPENDENT STATEHOOD.. 65

CHAPTER 35
THE SCIENTIFIC REVOLUTION AND ITS ENLIGHTENED AFTERMATH.. 67

CHAPTER 36
LIBERALISM AND THE CHALLENGE TO ABSOLUTIST MONARCHY... 69

CHAPTER 37
THE FRENCH REVOLUTION AND THE BONAPARTIST EMPIRE... 71

CHAPTER 38
EUROPE'S INDUSTRIALIZATION................................ 73

CHAPTER 39
THE SOCIAL IMPACTS OF EARLY INDUSTRY................ 75

CHAPTER 40
EUROPE IN IDEOLOGICAL CONFLICT........................... 77

CHAPTER 41
CONSOLIDATION OF NATIONAL STATES..................... 80

CHAPTER 42
ADVANCED INDUSTRIAL SOCIETY............................... 81

CHAPTER 43
MODERN SCIENCE AND ITS IMPLICATIONS.................. 84

CHAPTER 44
WORLD WAR I AND ITS DISPUTED SETTLEMENT......... 86

CHAPTER 45
A FRAGILE BALANCE: EUROPE, 1919-1929.................... 88

CHAPTER 46
THE SOVIET EXPERIMENT TO WORLD WAR II............. 90

CHAPTER 47
TOTALITARIANISM: THE NAZI STATE.......................... 93

CHAPTER 48
EAST ASIA IN A CENTURY OF CHANGE, 1840-1940.........95

CHAPTER 49
WORLD WAR II..................98

CHAPTER 50
HIGH AND LOW CULTURES IN THE WEST...................100

CHAPTER 51
SUPERPOWER RIVALRY AND THE EUROPEAN RECOVERY..................102

CHAPTER 52
DECOLONIZATION AND THE "THIRD WORLD"............105

CHAPTER 53
THE NEW ASIA................106

CHAPTER 54
AFRICA AFTER INDEPENDENCE................109

CHAPTER 55
LATIN AMERICA IN THE TWENTIETH CENTURY...........112

CHAPTER 56
THE REEMERGENCE OF THE MUSLIM WORLD..............115

CHAPTER 57
THE MARXIST COLLAPSE.............................117

CHAPTER 58
AT THE END OF THE TWENTIETH CENTURY.................120

PREFACE

Primary sources are the raw material of the historian's craft. Unlike natural scientists, historians cannot recreate "experimental" reality. But in order to be true to the past, they must attempt to get as close as possible to the past events and individuals they are studying. Primary sources are the means whereby historians do this. A primary source may be defined as anything contemporary with the event, person, or subject being studied. Thus, letters, government documents, photos, video tapes, artifacts, newspapers, diaries, and books are all examples of possible primary sources. We may not be able to revisit the world of the ancient Greeks, but reading their plays, their political debates, and studying their architecture are all examples of primary sources that bring that world closer to us. But the use of primary sources requires knowledge and interpretation on the part of the reader. A letter written from the front-line trenches by a British soldier in World War I may give us a vivid sense of the horrors and boredom of trench-warfare, but the soldier's knowledge of the overall scope of the war or the grand strategy of the generals was probably quite limited. The prejudices and limited knowledge of participants also have to be taken into account when using first-hand information, but it is precisely these prejudices and lack of knowledge that often make such sources so valuable. We should deplore the racism revealed in a speech made by a French politician in 1888 justifying the annexation of large parts of west Africa, but the value of such a speech is that it reveals commonly held opinions of that time and place, and it helps us to understand some of the motives for western imperialism. Thus, in using primary sources some basic knowledge of the period and place from which the source originated is essential. It is also essential to have some knowledge of the person or institution that created the source. With such background information, the historian and the student of history can then use primary sources to gain a clearer view of the reality of past events and people.

This reader is designed to be used with the world history text, WORLD CIVILIZATIONS, by Professor Adler, and other similar texts. The readings are designed to supplement the material presented in each chapter of the text. The documents presented and the questions asked are designed to be encountered after you have mastered the text material. Do not attempt to undertake the readings or answer the questions until you have completed reading the text chapter and successfully completing the TEST YOUR KNOWLEDGE self-test at the end of each chapter. In each chapter of this reader you will first encounter a brief description of the primary source that you are to read. Do not skip this section, for it will provide essential information necessary to understand the source. After each document, there will be a list of questions designed to guide you in your interpretation of the source. Some of these questions will be factual (i.e., what is being described?) and some will be interpretive (i.e., why is the author describing this event in this manner?). These interpretive questions will require you to engage in historical interpretation and hopefully will provide the basis of some class discussion. Good luck as you begin your quest for the truth about the past.

CHAPTER 1
PREHISTORY

Creation and origin stories are common to most ancient cultures. It appears that humans have an innate desire to make sense of their lives and surroundings by giving to themselves a distinguished heritage or having an account of their origins that identifies them with the gods. Composed and handed down orally for generations, many of these creation myths were later put into written form when writing was developed. But the North American Indian cultures and the West African cultures never developed written languages, so the only way we know many of these myths is through their recording by European traders and missionaries. The first selection below is a summary of the creation story of the Ottowa Indians of present day Canada. It was recorded in the memoirs of Nicolas Perrot in the seventeenth century. Perrot was a French Canadian trader, missionary, and government agent to the Ottowa and other tribes of the Great Lakes region. He admired the Indians and took great pains to record their history and myths as they were told to him. The second selection is from a series of origin tales of the Luba people of central Africa and was recorded by European anthropologists in the early twentieth century. Although from times and places far removed from the much earlier creation myths of Asia, the following stories have many elements found in creation myths from most early societies, and also account for the social roles of men and women.

CREATION MYTH OF THE OTTOWA

After the creation of the earth, all the other animals withdrew into the places which each kind found most suitable for obtaining their pasture or their prey. When the first ones died, the Great Hare caused the birth of men from their corpses, as also from those of the fishes which were found along the shores of the rivers which he had formed in creating the land. Accordingly, some of the savages derive their origin from a bear, others a moose, and others similarly from various kinds of animals; … their villages each bear the name of the animal which has given its people their being- as that of the crane, or the bear, or of other animals … These first men … whom hunger had weakened, inspired by the Great Hare … broke off a branch from a small tree, made a cord with the fibers of the nettles … and thus they formed a bow and arrows with which they killed small birds. After that, they made crossbow arrows in order to attack the large beasts; they skinned these, and tried to eat the flesh. But as they found only the fat savory, they tried to make fire, in order to cook their meat … The skins of the animals served for their covering … They invented a sort of racket in order to walk on the snow with more ease; and they constructed canoes, in order to enable them to cross the rivers … These men … while hunting found the footprints of an enormously tall man … This colossus, having wakened, said, " My son, why art thou afraid? Reassure thyself; I am the Great Hare, he who has caused thee and many others to be born from the dead bodies of various animals. Now I will give thee a companion." Here are the words that he used in giving the man a wife: "Thou man," said he, " shalt hunt, and make canoes, and do all things that a man must do; and thou, woman, shalt do the cooking for thy husband, make his shoes, dress the skins of animals, sew, and perform all the tasks that are proper for a woman."

A BANTU MYTH OF MIGRATION

In the country of the east, on the right bank of the Lualaba River, there once was a man and a woman. Their names mean respectively "he who builds many houses" and "she who makes much pottery." They lived in ignorance of each other. Guided by the sound of chopping, the man discovered the woman, who was preparing firewood. They lived for a long time under the same roof, sleeping in separate beds. The copulation of a pair of jackals gave them the idea of sleeping together. They brought forth twins of opposite sex, who became inseparable companions. One day the twins found a locality that was exceptionally rich in fish. They finally obtained permission from their parents to leave the village and devote themselves entirely to fishing. In their turn, they brought forth twins, who lived in the same incestuous manner, far from their parents. This new generation took up trapping. So pairs of twins, moving each generation a little farther westward, populated the country.

TEXTUAL QUESTIONS FOR ANALYSIS

1. What are the similarities and differences in each account of the origins of men and women?
2. How does each account deal with the role of women and men?
3. Are there any similarities in these accounts with other creation accounts with which you are familiar? What appears to be the common themes of all creation accounts?

Source: James Axtell, ed. *The Indian Peoples of Eastern America: A Documentary History of the Sexes* (New York: Oxford University Press, 1981), pp. 180-181. Luc de Heusch, *The Drunken King or the Origin of the State* (Bloomington: Indiana University Press, 1982), pp. 11-12.

CHAPTER 2
MESOPOTAMIA

~ 1750 BC

The law code of Hammurabi is not the oldest from Mesopotamia, but it is the most complete. The code is probably most known for its concept of retribution, an "eye for an eye." But most of its provisions deal with economic issues, such as contracts, and family and property issues. At the time Hammurabi proclaimed his code, he had created an empire, centered in Babylon, that stretched from the Persian Gulf to the headwaters of the Tigris and Euphrates rivers. His code (consisting of a Prologue and 282 specific laws) was written on stone pillars and erected in the major cities of his empire. The code reveals a concept of justice that is surprisingly modern, a religious justification for the legal authority of the king, and an urban and commercial society. It also reveals a society in which the concept of rights and penalties is clearly based on class and sex.

HAMMURABI'S CODE
PROLOGUE

When the lofty Anu...and Enlil, lords of heaven and earth...committed the rule of all mankind to Marduk...at that time Anu and Enlil named me, Hammurabi, the exalted prince, the worshipper of the gods, to cause righteousness to prevail in the land, to destroy the wicked and the evil, to prevent the strong from plundering the weak...to enlighten the land and to further the welfare of the people...

3. If a man has borne false witness in a trial, or has not established the statement that he has made, if that cause be a capital crime, that man shall be put to death. **5.** If a judge has given a verdict, rendered a decision, granted a written judgment, and afterward has altered his judgment, that judge shall be prosecuted for altering the judgment he gave and shall pay twelve-fold the penalty laid down in that judgment. Further, he shall be publicly expelled from his judgment-seat and shall not return nor take his seat with the judges at a trial. **6.** If a man has stolen goods from a temple, or house, he shall be put to death; and he that has received the stolen property from him shall be put to death. **8.** If a nobleman has stolen ox, sheep, ass, pig, or ship, whether from temple or a house, he shall pay thirty-fold. If he be a commoner, he shall return ten-fold. If the thief cannot pay, he shall be put to death. **22.** If a man has committed highway robbery and has been caught, that man shall be put to death. **23.** If the highwayman has not been caught, the man that has been robbed shall state on oath what he has lost and the city or district governor in whose territory the robbery took place shall restore to him what he has lost. **129.** If a man's wife is caught lying with another, they shall be strangled and cast into the water. If the wife's husband would save his wife, the king can save his servant. **131.** If a man's wife has been accused by her husband, and has not been caught lying with another, she shall swear her innocence, and return to her house. **134.** If a man has been taken captive, and there was maintenance in his house, but his wife has left his house and entered into another man's house; because that woman has not preserved her body, and has entered into the house of another, that woman shall be prosecuted and shall be drowned. **135.** If a man has been taken captive, but there was not maintenance in his house, and his wife has entered into the house of another, that woman has no blame. **136.** If a man has left his city and fled and after he has gone his wife has entered into the house of another, if the man returns and seizes his wife, the wife of the fugitive shall not return to her husband because he hated his city and fled. **138.** If a man has divorced his wife, who has not borne him children, he shall pay over to her as much money as was given for her bride-price and the dowry which she brought from her father's house, and so shall divorce her. **148.** If a man has married a wife and disease has seized her, if he is determined to marry a second wife, he shall marry her. He shall not divorce the wife whom the disease seized. In the home they made together she shall dwell, and he shall maintain her as long as she lives. **195.** If a son has struck his father, his hands shall be cut off. **196.** If a nobleman has destroyed the eye of another nobleman. his own eye shall be destroyed. **197.** If a nobleman has broken the bone of another nobleman, his own bone shall be broken. **198.** If a nobleman has destroyed the eye of a peasant or broken the bone of a peasant he shall pay one mina of silver. **199.** If a nobleman has destroyed the eye of a man's slave, or broken the bone of a man's slave, he shall pay half the value of the slave. **200.** If a man has knocked out the teeth of a man of the same rank, his own teeth shall be knocked out. **202.** If a man strikes the body of a man who is superior in status, he shall publicly receive sixty lashes with a cowhide whip. **215.** If a surgeon has operated with a bronze lancet on a nobleman for a serious injury, and has cured him, or has removed with a bronze lancet a cataract for a nobleman, and has cured his eye, he shall pay ten shekels of silver. **215.** If it be a commoner, he shall take five shekels of silver. **216.** If it be a man's slave, the owner of the slave shall give two shekels of silver to the surgeon. **229.** If a builder has built a house for a man, and has not made his work sound, and the house he built has fallen, and caused the death of the owner, that builder shall be put to death. **230.** If it is the owner's son that is killed, the builder's son shall be put to death. **232.** If he has caused the loss of goods, he shall render back whatever he has destroyed. Moreover, because he did not make sound the house he built, and it fell, at his own cost he shall rebuild the house that fell.

TEXTUAL QUESTIONS FOR ANALYSIS

1. According to Hammurabi, what is the origin and purpose of government and law? How does this compare with the stated origin and purpose of government and law as found in the preamble to the U.S. Constitution?
2. What evidence is there for class and legal distinctions in this society?
3. What is the apparent status of women in this society? Are there any protections for women provided by the code?
4. What protection does the law provide for consumers?
5. The concept of "an eye for an eye" that comes from this law code is used today to describe any legal system that is notable for its severity. Is this law code simply severe or is there an attempt to provide fairness? Explain.

Source: J. M. Powis-Smith, *The Origin and History of Hebrew Law* (Chicago: University of Chicago Prss, 1960), pp. 183, 185-186.

CHAPTER 3
EGYPT

As your text points out, the Egyptians from very early in their history had a great concern with the afterlife. In the period of the Old Kingdom, only the pharaoh and his family were considered eligible for immortality, but by the Middle Kingdom life after death was considered possible for high status individuals, with the important provision that they had to merit immortality by their ethical conduct during this life. Egyptian priests developed the concept of a judgment by the gods that took place after death in which an individual had to face Osiris, god of the underworld. There he had to justify his request for immortality by making declarations of his good conduct, his religious zeal, and listing a host of evil actions that he had not done. By the time of the New Kingdom, the concept of immortality had been extended downward to include anyone that had led an ethical life, and could afford some type of godly preservation after death. THE BOOK OF THE DEAD is the name given by modern scholars to a series of mortuary texts that were compiled during the Middle and New Kingdom periods of Egyptian history. They were written on papyrus rolls, typically with extensive art work showing the deceased and his family, his good works, and the process of judgment in which his soul was weighed against an ostrich feather. The papyrus rolls would be inserted in the coffin of the deceased and were intended as a sort of letter of introduction or court brief that the deceased would be able to use in his encounter with the gods during the process of judgment in the afterlife. Written by priests, no doubt at considerable expense, hundreds of these have been found, and if all Egyptians behaved as well as these texts indicate, it would surely have been the most peaceful and benevolent society ever seen. The value of these texts is that they provide us with a good view of the ideals, manners, and values of ancient Egypt. These texts show us how the Egyptians wanted to behave, and what they considered a good life, not how they really conducted their daily lives. The following example is from the 16th century B.C.E., and is a standard formula in which a blank space was provided for the insertion of the name of the deceased (indicated here by "X").

THE BOOK OF THE DEAD

What is said on reaching the Broad-Hall of the Two Justices, absolving X of every sin which he has committed, and seeing the faces of the gods:

Hail to thee, O great god, lord of the Two Justices! I have come to thee, my lord, I have been brought that I might see thy beauty. I know thee; I know thy name and the names of the forty-two gods who are with thee in the Broad-Hall of the Two Justices, who live on them who preserve evil and who drink their blood on the day of reckoning... In truth I have come to thee and I have destroyed wickedness for thee. I have not committed evil against men. I have not oppressed the members of my family. I have not mistreated cattle. I have not blasphemed a god. I have not done violence to a poor man. I have not done that which the gods abominate. I have not defamed a slave to his superior. I have not made anyone sick. I have not made anyone weep. I have not murdered. I have not ordered anyone murdered. I have not reduced the income of the temples. I have not taken the offerings of the dead. I have not had sexual relations with a boy. I have not defiled myself. I have not taken milk from the mouths of children. I have not driven cattle away from their pasturage. I have not dammed up the water when it should flow. I have not encroached upon the fields of others. I have not neglected the times of offering to the gods. I have not built a dam against running water. I am pure! I am pure! I am pure! I am pure!....

TEXTUAL QUESTIONS FOR ANALYSIS

1. Egyptian society obviously had a strongly developed concept of correct conduct. What are some of the things that a righteous person should do? What are some of the sins that a person should avoid?
2. In what ways do these Egyptian ideas of correct behavior resemble our own and in what ways do they differ?
3. What are the consequences of evil behavior according to the text? Could such texts have been of value to the living?
4. By the time of the New Kingdom, an afterlife of bliss was in theory available to all who had lived an ethical life. Mummification and the purchase of these texts was, however, expensive. What do these facts tell us about the social reality of ancient Egyptian life and the prospects of the poor in hoping to attain an afterlife of reward?

Source: Miriam Lichtheim, ed., *Ancient Egyptian Literature, A Book of Readings* (Los

Angeles: University of California Press, 1976), Vol. 2, pp. 124-126.

CHAPTER 4
EMPIRES AND THEOLOGY IN THE NEAR EAST: PERSIANS AND JEWS

One of the most important legacies of the Persians is the religion known as Zoroastrianism, founded according to tradition by a religious prophet named Zarathustra, and established as the official religion of the Persian royal family by the Emperor Darius I (558-486 B.C.E.). The accepted details about the life of Zarathustra are few. It is believed that he was a Persian, that he lived in the seventh century, that he led a wandering life seeking spiritual enlightenment, that his life as a prophet led to the beginnings of Zoroastrianism, and that he recorded his religious revelations in a series of hymns that later became the sacred canon of scripture known as the Avesta. As your text points out, Zoroastrianism is considered to have had an influence on both Judaism and Christianity, although scholars still disagree about the precise degree of influence due to the lack of information about the actual life and career of Zarathustra or Zoroaster. The Avesta is divided into many hymns, or "Yasnas," of which the Gathas are the most ancient. These earliest hymns are considered the most likely to have been composed by Zarathustra, and they emphasize the ethical nature of his religious ideals and the type of spiritual revelations he experienced.

THE GATHAS OF ZOROASTER

Yasna Thirty—Hear with your ears the best things. Look upon them with clear-seeing thought for a decision between the two Beliefs, each man for himself must make before the Great Consummation... Now the two primal Spirits, who revealed themselves in a vision as Twins, are the Better and the Bad in thought and word and action. And between these two the wise once chose aright, the foolish not so. And when these two Spirits came together in the beginning, they established Life and Death, so that at the last the Worst Existence shall be given to the followers of the Lie, but the Best Thought or dwelling shall be given to him that follows Right. Of these two Spirits he that followed the Lie chose doing the worst things. The holiest Spirits chose right... so likewise they that are glad to please Ahura Mazda by dutiful actions... If you mortals, you mark those commandments that Mazda has ordained—of happiness and pain, the long punishment for the liars, and blessings for the righteous—then hereafter shall you have bliss.

Yasna Thirty-one—I conceived of you, oh Ahura Mazda, in my thought that you, the First, are also the Last—that you are Father of Good Thought, for thus I apprehended You with my eye—that you did truly create Right, and are the Lord to judge the actions of life... When you, Mazda, in the beginning did create beings and men by your Thought, and intelligences—when you did make life clothed with body, when you made actions and teachings, whereby one may exercise choice according to one's free will: then liftest up his voice the false speaker or the true speaker... Whether is greater, the belief of the righteous or of the liar? Let him that knows tell him that does not know; let not him that knows nothing deceive any more. Be to us, oh Ahura Mazda, the teacher of Good Thought. Let none of you listen to the liar's words and commands: he brings house and clan and district and land into misery and destruction. Resist them then with weapons!... Whoso comes to the righteous one, far from him shall be the future long age of misery, of darkness, ill food, and crying of woe! To such an existence, you liars, shall your own self bring you by your actions....

TEXTUAL QUSTIONS FOR ANALYSIS

1. According to Zoroaster, what is the source of evil in the world and what is the solution to the problem of evil?
2. What is promised to those that act with goodness and to those that do not act with goodness?
3. Which of the two forces is the stronger according to Zoroaster? What do you think he means by the "Great Consummation" in Yasna Thirty?
4. What similarities do you see in this brief selection between Zoroastrianism and Judaism and Christianity? How do you account for these similarities?

Source: James Hope Moulton, *Early Zoroastrianism* (London: Williams and Norgate, 1913), pp. 350-354.

CHAPTER 5
INDIA'S BEGINNINGS

India is the home of two of the world's great religious systems, Hinduism and Buddhism. Hinduism developed from the merging of the traditional religious system of the native Indians and the nature gods of the Invading Aryans. This process began with the invasion of the Aryans about 1500 B.C.E. and continued for hundreds of years as the Aryan priests, the Brahmins, developed an extensive oral literature centered on elaborate sacrificial rituals. These earliest religious rituals, chants, and hymns were collected into the Vedas. Between about 700 and 500 B.C.E. Hindu priests went beyond the early concepts of the caste system and the other concerns of the Vedas to produce another great body of religious literature, the Upanishads. The term means "additional sitting near a teacher," and the texts, originally handed down orally just like the Vedas, often took the form of a dialogue between a student and master. In the Upanishads, the Brahmin teachers developed the idea of an all-encompassing deity, Brahman, whose essence could be found in everyone. The inner most self of a person, his atman, was one with Brahman: thus humans are not outside of ultimate Divinity, they are part of it. The following selection from the Upanishads shows how Hindu masters sought to convey this spiritual concept to their students. Buddhism began as a reform movement within Hinduism when the Kshatriya prince, Siddharta Gautama, broke with traditional Hindu teachings in the 6th century B.C.E. and created a communal religious movement based on individual enlightenment that rejected the caste system and the numerous Hindu deities. The Buddha, as he soon came to be known to his followers, accepted traditional Hindu concepts of reincarnation and individual responsibility for one's ultimate fate, but he emphasized a "middle way" between extreme self-denial and extreme self-indulgence as the true path to "nirvana." This was the world's first missionary religion, for the Buddhist scriptures record that after he achieved his enlightenment, his first action was to go and find his fellow religious ascetics, and preach the new doctrine to them. He then founded a monastic order which would provide a model to the rest of the world of a proper religious life. The selection that follows is a portion of Buddha's first sermon from the Pali Canon, the earliest Buddhist scripture, in which the Enlightened One first reveals the Four Noble Truths and the Eightfold Path.

THE UPANISHADS

There once lived Svetaketu.... To him his father Uddalaka said: "Svetaketu, go to school; no one belonging to our race, dear son, who, not having studied, is a Brahmin by birth only." Having begun his apprenticeship when he was twelve years of age, Svetaketu returned to his father when he was twenty-four, having studied all the Vedas—conceited, considering himself well-read and stern. His father said to him: "Svetaketu, as you are so conceited.... Have you ever asked for that instruction by which we perceive what cannot be perceived, by which we know what cannot be known?"
"What is that instruction, Sir?" he asked....
"Fetch me.... a fruit of the Nyagrodha tree."
"Here is one, Sir."
"Break it."
"It is broken, Sir."
"What do you see there?"
"These seeds, almost infinitesimal."
"Break one of them."
"It is broken, Sir."
"What do you see there?"
"Not anything, Sir."

The father said: "My son, that subtle essence which you do not perceive there, of that very essence this great Nyagrodha tree exists. Believe it, my son. That which is the subtle essence, in it all that exists has its self. It is the True. It is the Self, and you, my son, are it."

THE BUDDHA'S FIRST SERMON

And the Blessed one thus addressed the five Bhikkhus (the five religious ascetics that had been with Buddha in the forest), "There are two extremes.... which he who has given up the world ought to avoid. What are these two extremes? A life given to pleasures, devoted to pleasures and lusts: this is degrading, sensual, vulgar, ignoble, and profitless; and a life given to mortifications: this is painful, ignoble and profitless. By avoiding these two extremes One who has arrived at the Truth has gained the knowledge of the Middle Path which leads to insight, which leads to wisdom which conduces to calm. to knowledge.... to Nirvana."
"Which.... is the Middle Path.... which leads to insight, which leads to wisdom, which conduces to calm, to knowledge.... to Nirvana? It is the Holy Eightfold Path, namely, Right Belief, Right Aspiration, Right Speech, Right Conduct, Right Means of Livelihood, Right Endeavor, Right Contemplation, Right Mediation...." "This.... is the Noble Truth of suffering.... clinging to existence is suffering.... This is the Noble Truth of the cause of suffering.... Thirst for pleasure, thirst for existence, thirst for prosperity is the cause of suffering.... This.... is the Noble Truth of the cessation of suffering: it ceases with the

complete cessation of this thirst—a cessation which ceases with the destruction of desire by the Holy Eightfold Path."

TEXTUAL QUESTIONS FOR ANALYSIS

1. State in your own words the essential teaching in the above section of the Upanishads. Is this an idea that can be found in other religions?
2. State in your own words the essential teaching in the above selection from Buddha's first sermon? Are these concepts found in other religions?
3. From your reading in the text and the above selections, describe the major differences between Hinduism and Buddhism.
4. What was the attraction of Buddhism in the India of Buddha's day? What do you think would be Buddha's opinion of modern American culture, and what would he recommend?

Source: Allie M. Frazier, ed., *Readings in Eastern Religious Thought* (Philadelphia: Westminster Press, 1969), Vol. 1, pp. 135-136.

CHAPTER 6
ANCIENT CHINA TO 500 B.C.E

Confucius is considered to be one of the most influential Chinese philosophers of the classical age. He believed that through proper education in ancient literature and the cultivation of proper behavior and humane conduct, young men could become gentlemen, or as he termed it "superior man." His teachings were preserved after his death in the ANALECTS, one of the most influential books in world history. For two thousand years, young Chinese scholars studied and memorized the ANALECTS in order to improve themselves and to qualify for a post in the imperial bureaucracy. The ANALECTS are written in the form of questions and answers and maxims that Confucius gave to his pupils concerning questions of morality and proper conduct. We do not know which of them are the actual words of Confucius and which were added by later disciples, but collectively they provide us the best record we have of the thoughts and life of Master Kung.

THE ANALECTS

Zi asked the Master what was filial piety? The Master said, "The filial piety of today means the support of one's parents. But dogs and horses likewise are able to do something in the way of support. Without reverence, what is there to distinguish the one support given from the other?"

The Master said, "In serving his parents, a son may remonstrate with them, but gently; when he sees that they do not incline to follow his advice, he shows an increased degree of reverence, but does not abandon his purpose; and should they punish him, he does not allow himself to murmur."

The Master said, "When rulers love to observe the rules of propriety, the people respond readily to the calls on them for service."

The Master said, "He who exercises government by means of his virtue may be compared to the north polar star, which keeps its place and all the stars turn towards it."

The Duke Ai asked, saying, "What should be done in order to secure the submission of the people?" Confucius replied, "Advance the upright and set aside the crooked, then the people will submit. Advance the crooked and set aside the upright, then the people will not submit."

Ji Kang asked how to cause the people to reverence their ruler, to be faithful to him, and to aspire to virtue? The Master said, "Let him preside over them with gravity; then they will reverence him. Let him be filial and kind to all; then they will be faithful to him. Let him advance the good and teach the incompetent; then they will eagerly seek to be virtuous."

The Master said, "If a minister make his own conduct correct, what difficulty will he have in assisting in government? If he cannot rectify himself, what has he to do with rectifying others?"

Zi Gong asked what constituted the superior man? The Master said, "He acts before he speaks, and afterward speaks according to his actions."

The Master said, "The mind of the superior man is conversant with righteousness; the mind of the common man is conversant with gain."

The Master said, "By extensively studying all learning, and keeping himself under the restraint of the rules of propriety, one may thus not err from what is right."

Ji Lu asked about serving the spirits of the dead? The Master said, "While you are not able to serve men, how can you serve their spirits?" Ji Lu added, "I venture to ask about death?" The Master answered, "While you do not know life, how can you know about death?"

TEXTUAL QUESTIONS FOR ANALYSIS

1. From the above, what would you say were the major concerns of Confucius? Would you say that his concerns were secular or spiritual?
2. Would you say that Confucius believed that government was important or unimportant in the lives of the people? What did he see as the proper role of government?
3. Does Confucius make any distinction between public and private morality for government leaders? What do you think would be his opinion of modern American politics?
4. Define what Confucius meant by filial piety. Why do you think he considered it the most essential of all virtues?

Source: James R. Ware, ed. and trans., *The Sayings of Confucius* (New York: Mentor Books, 1955), pp. 26-28

CHAPTER 7
ORDINARY LIVES IN THE ANCIENT PAST

Most of the information concerning the lives of individuals that we possess from the ancient world concerns the rich, the powerful, and the well-born. Written records from most of the ancient civilizations seldom deal with the lives of the great majority of the population, the peasants and the craftsmen who performed most of the work and paid most of the taxes. But there are written records from Egypt that provide a partial glimpse into the lives of the common people. The profession of scribe was one of the most honored and difficult in ancient Egypt. Learning the complex hieroglyphic form of writing took years of practice and memorization. Writing was taught by practicing scribes in schools known as the "House of Life." Young students would spend years learning to write by copying lessons prepared for them by the senior scribes. If they succeeded in mastering the craft, the rewards were great- steady and well-rewarded employment for the rest of their lives, either as government or priestly scribes, or as independent scribes working for individuals. Thousands of the practice lessons that young scribes completed have been preserved as papyrus scrolls, writing tablets, and shards of pottery. The following selection is a writing exercise completed by a young student in the time of the late New Kingdom (about 1200 B.C.E.). His teacher wrote a lesson designed to provide encouragement for his pupil by outlining the hard life of other trades and crafts. The copy exercise also offers to us a close look at the hard life of ordinary people of 3000 years ago in the Nile valley.

PAPYRUS LANSING: A SCHOOL BOOK

Nebmare-nakht, the royal scribe and chief overseer of the cattle of Amen-Re, King of the Gods, speaks to the apprentice scribe Wenemdiamun. Apply yourself to this noble profession... You will find it useful...You will be advanced by your superiors. Love writing, shun dancing; then you become a worthy official. Do not long for the birds and fish of the marsh. Turn your back on the throw stick and chase. By day write with your fingers; recite by night. Befriend the scroll, the palette. It pleases more than wine. Writing for him who knows it is better than all other professions. It pleases more than bread and beer, more than clothing and ointment. It is worth more than an inheritance....

See for yourself with your eye. The occupations lie before you. The washerman's day is going up, going down. All his limbs are weak from whitening his neighbor's clothes every day, from washing their linen. The maker of pots is smeared with soil, like one whose relations have died. His hands, his feet, are full of clay; he is like one who lives in the bog. The cobbler mingles with vats. His odor is penetrating. His hands are red with madder, like one who is smeared with blood. He looks behind him for the kite, like one whose flesh is exposed. The watchman prepares garlands and polishes vase-stands. He spends a night of toil just as one on whom the sun shines. The merchants travel downstream and upstream. They are as busy as can be, carrying goods from one town to another. They supply him who has wants. But the tax collectors carry off the gold, that most precious of metals. The ships' crews receive their loads from every house of commerce. They depart from Egypt for Syria, and each man's god is with him. But not one of them says, "We shall see Egypt again!" The carpenter who is in the shipyard carries the timber and stacks it. If he gives today the output of yesterday, woe to his limbs! The shipwright stands behind him to tell him evil things. His outworker who is in the fields, his is the toughest of all the jobs. He spends the day loaded with his tools, tied to his toolbox. When he returns home at night, he is loaded with the toolbox and the timbers, his drinking mug, and his whetstones. The scribe, he alone, records the output of all of them. Take note of it!

Come, let me tell you the woes of the soldier, and how many are his superiors.... He is called up for Syria. He may not rest. There are no clothes, no sandals. His march is uphill through mountains. He drinks water every third day.... His body is ravaged with illness. The enemy comes, surrounds him with missiles, and life recedes from him.... His wife and children are in their village; he dies and does not reach it.... He dies on the edge of the desert, and there is none to perpetuate his name.... He does not know his resting place. Be a scribe, and be spared from soldiering.... You are safe from torments.... You stride about inspecting.... You are dressed in fine clothes; you own horses. Your boat is on the river.... You have a powerful office, given you by the king.... If you have any sense, be a scribe!

TEXTUAL QUESTIONS FOR ANALYSIS

1. Briefly summarize the argument used here to encourage the young student to continue his studies to become a scribe. What are the common unattractive aspects of the other crafts and trades summarized here?
2. Why would the fate of the soldier be particularly unattractive to an Egyptian of the New Kingdom?
3. Does the advice of the teacher scribe sound like any advice you may have heard before? Where?

Source: Miriam Lichtheim, ed., *Ancient Egyptian Literature, A Book of Readings* (Los Angeles: University of California Press, 1976), Vol. 2, pp. 169-172.

CHAPTER 8
THE GREEK ADVENTURE

The Greeks invented the concept of writing history as a record of human characters acting within a social, political, and economic framework, rather than simply recording past events as the will of the gods. One of the best of the ancient Greek historians was Thucydides, an aristocratic citizen of Athens who lived from about 470 to about 400 B.C.E. He was a contemporary of Pericles, a descendant of Miltiades (the victor of Marathon), and a soldier in the Peloponnesian War. After he failed in defending an allied city from a Spartan force early in the war, he was sent into exile by the Athenians for twenty years. He spent the years of his exile investigating and writing about this conflict, which he believed was a disaster for all Greeks, and especially Athenians and Spartans. He believed that wars were the result of human actions and choices, and that if people were acquainted with the causes of war, they might avoid such calamities in the future. Thus, he wrote his famous history with a view to preventing such mistakes being made again. The following brief selection from his lengthy account is from the funeral oration of Pericles of Athens. Thucydides may well have been present at the occasion of the ceremony, but he did not try to give a verbatim account of the speeches of famous individuals, but only to "put into the mouth of each speaker the sentiments proper to the occasion, expressed as I thought he would be likely to express them..." The occasion of the speech was a state funeral at the end of the first year of the war, during which all the soldiers killed during that first campaign were honored. Remember that Pericles was an elected official who was not only honoring fallen warriors, but also attempting to justify the war, to explain the sacrifices demanded by the war, to call for continued sacrifices, and comparing Athens to its opponent, Sparta.

HISTORY OF THE PELOPONNESIAN WAR—PERICLES'S FUNERAL SPEECH

I will speak first of our ancestors, for it is right and becoming that now, when we are lamenting the dead, a tribute should be paid to their memory. There has never been a time when they did not inhabit this land, which by their valor they have handed down from generation to generation, and we have received from them a free state.... Before I praise the dead, I should like to point out by what principles of action we rose to power, and under what institutions and through what manner of life our empire became great. For I conceive that such thoughts are not unsuited to the occasion, and that this numerous assembly of citizens and strangers may profitably listen to them.

Our form of government does not enter into rivalry with the institutions of others. We do not copy our neighbors, but are an example to them. It is true that we are called a democracy, for the administration is in the hands of the many and not of the few. But while the law secures equal justice to all alike in their private disputes, the claim of excellence is also recognized; and when a citizen is in any way distinguished, he is preferred to the public service, not as a matter of privilege, but as the reward of merit. Neither is poverty a bar, but a man may benefit his country whatever be the obscurity of his condition.... A spirit of reverence pervades our public acts; we are prevented from doing wrong by respect for authority and the laws, having an especial regard to those which are ordained for the protection of the injured as well as those unwritten laws which bring upon the transgressor of them the reprobation of the general sentiment.

And we have not forgotten to provide for our weary spirits many relaxations from toil; we have regular games and sacrifices throughout the year; at home the style of our life is refined; and the delight which we daily feel in all these things helps to banish melancholy. Because of the greatness of our city the fruits of the whole earth flow in upon us, so that we enjoy the goods of other countries as freely as of our own.

Then, again, our military training is in many respects superior to that of our adversaries. Our city is thrown open to the world, and we never expel a foreigner or prevent him from seeing or learning anything of which the secret if revealed to an enemy might profit him. We rely not upon management or trickery, but upon our own hearts and hands. And in the matter of education, whereas they (i.e. the Spartans) from early youth are always undergoing laborious exercises which are to make them brave, we live at ease, and yet are equally ready to face the perils which they face....

If we then prefer to meet danger with a light heart but without laborious training, and with a courage which is gained by habit and not enforced by law, are we not greatly the gainers?.... For we are lovers of the beautiful, yet simple in our tastes, and we cultivate the mind without loss of manliness. Wealth we employ, not for talk or ostentation, but when there is a real use for it. To avow poverty with us is no disgrace; the true disgrace is in doing nothing to avoid it. An Athenian citizen does not neglect the state because he takes care of his own household; and even those of us who are engaged in business have a very fair idea of politics. We alone regard a man who takes no interest in public affairs, not as harmless, but as a useless character....

To sum up: I say that Athens is the school of Hellas, and that the individual Athenian in his own person seems to have the power of adapting himself to the most varied forms of action with the utmost versatility and grace.... For in the hour of trial Athens alone among her contemporaries is superior to the report of her.... Such is the city for whose sake these men nobly fought and died; they could not bear the thought that she might be taken from them; and every one of us who survive should gladly toil on her behalf....

TEXTUAL QUESTIONS FOR ANALYSIS

1. Does this speech sound like a speech a modern political leader might make? Explain your answer.
2. What are the qualities that make Athens a great city according to Pericles? What is expected of every citizen?
3. Pericles unfavorably compares Sparta, directly and indirectly, to Athens. In what areas does he consider Sparta inferior to Athens?
4. Relative to the rest of Greece, what is Athens according to Pericles? Why should the citizens not lose heart and what does Athens expect of every citizen?

Source: Thucydides, *History of the Peloponnesian War,* trans. Richard Crawley (London: J. M. Dent and Co., 1903), Vol. 1, pp. 120-128.

CHAPTER 9
HELLENIC CULTURE

In addition to the great works of literature and philosophy produced by the Greeks, a great body of popular literature was also produced, much of which has been lost. But the stories of Aesop were preserved, and have become part of our cultural heritage. Most people have heard of the tortoise and the hare, and many know the story itself; what they might not realize is that the story is about 2500 years old, and is part of the legacy of Greek culture. Aesop is a semi-legendary figure who supposedly lived about 620-560 B.C.E. Hundreds of fables were ascribed to him, and a large collection compiled in the late fifth century B.C.E. and attributed to him forms the basis of what we today know as Aesop's FABLES. The most widely accepted version of his life is that he was a slave whose ability as a storyteller led to his being granted his freedom. Many scholars doubt that there was a single individual named Aesop who composed all of the stories, but that the fables were the work of many individuals, handed down orally over a long period of time, and when compiled were attributed to this legendary figure with the gift of tale-telling. The FABLES are presented in the form of short stories, most of which feature animals that act like humans. Most of the stories are quite short, usually only a few sentences or paragraphs in length, and they all end with the statement of the moral, so the hearer is sure to get the point. They are noted for their humor, irony, and psychological insights into human nature. They remain as interesting for adults and children today as they probably were 2500 years ago for the ancient Greeks.

AESOP'S FABLES

THE WOLF IN SHEEP'S CLOTHING

A Wolf found great difficulty in getting at the sheep owing to the vigilance of the shepherd and his dogs. But one day it found the skin of a sheep that had been flayed and thrown aside, so it put it on over its own pelt and strolled down among the sheep. The Lamb of that sheep, whose skin the Wolf was wearing, began to follow the Wolf in sheep's clothing; so, leading the Lamb a little apart, the Wolf soon made a meal of her, and for some time he succeeded in deceiving the sheep, and enjoying hearty meals.
APPEARANCES ARE DECEPTIVE.

THE FOX AND THE GRAPES

One hot summer day a Fox was strolling through an orchard till he came to a bunch of grapes just ripening on a vine which had been trained over a lofty branch. "Just the thing to quench my thirst," said he. Drawing back a few paces, he took a run and a jump, and just missed the bunch. Turning around again with One, Two, Three, he jumped again, but with no greater success. Again and again, he tried after the tempting morsel, but at last had to give it up, and walked away with his nose in the air, saying, "I am sure they are sour."
IT IS EASY TO DESPISE WHAT YOU CANNOT GET.

THE GOOSE WITH THE GOLDEN EGGS

One day a countryman going to the nest of his Goose found there an egg all yellow and glittering. When he took it up it was heavy as lead and he was going to throw it away, because he thought a trick had been played upon him. But he took it home on second thought, and soon found to his delight that it was an egg of pure gold. Every morning the same thing occurred, and he soon became rich by selling his eggs. As he grew rich he grew greedy; and thinking to get at once all the gold the Goose could give, he killed it and opened it only to find- nothing.
GREED OFTEN OVERREACHES ITSELF.

THE OLD MAN AND DEATH

An old laborer, bent double with age and toil, was gathering sticks in a forest. At last he grew so tired and hopeless that he threw down the bundle of sticks and cried out: "I cannot bear this life any longer. Ah, I wish Death would only come and take me!"

As he spoke, Death, a grisly skeleton, appeared and said to him, "What wouldst thou, Mortal? I heard thee call me."

"Please sir," replied the woodcutter, "would you kindly help me to lift this bundle of sticks on to my shoulder?"
WE WOULD OFTEN BE SORRY IF OUR WISHES WERE GRATIFIED.

TEXTUAL QUESTIONS FOR ANALYSIS

1. What do you think contributes to the continuing popularity of these stories after 2000 years?
2. What do these stories tell us about ancient Greek society?
3. Most of these stories were probably memorized and repeated orally, passing from generation to generation before they were written down. How might this have changed the way they developed?
5. Many of these characters are animals rather than humans. Why do you think this technique was used? How might this affect the way the stories were read and interpreted?

Source: Donald S. Gochbert, ed., *Classics of Ancient Thought: The Ancient World*, 4th ed. (New York: Harcourt Brace Jovanovich, 1988), Vol. 1, pp. 40-46.

CHAPTER 10
HELLENISTIC CIVILIZATION

Alexander the Great perplexed his contemporaries and continues to puzzle scholars today. Was he a visionary statesman, committed to establishing a political system that would maintain the best of both Greek and Persian institutions, or was he simply a tyrant who ruthlessly pursued his own glory? Both interpretations, and several in between, had their champions in the ancient world, and the question of Alexander's goals, motives, and ultimate objectives is still debated today. His career is the very stuff of controversy: a young, talented ruler that took on one of the world's great empires, conquered it through brilliant military tactics, marched all the way to the borders of India, and died at the very moment of his triumph. What has contributed to the controversy regarding his personality and motives is that our sources for his life and career are all from later periods. The contemporary accounts of his Persian conquest, written by scholars that accompanied his army, exist only in fragments. The best ancient account of Alexander's life is that of the Greek historian Arrian of the second century C.E., over four hundred years after the events being described. His account is based on some of the eyewitness accounts that are now lost, but even so there are numerous questions about Alexander that Arrian does not answer. The selection that follows is from Arrian's THE LIFE OF ALEXANDER THE GREAT. This passage deals with events that took place near the end of Alexander's incredible journey of conquest. The year was 324 B.C.E., and Alexander had assembled his Macedonian troops near the city of Opis in Mesopotamia. He announced that he planned to lavishly reward and send home all Macedonian troops that were disabled or too old to continue as soldiers. But the entire army began to clamor to be sent home, and Alexander reacted with anger, arrested the ringleaders. He then spoke to the army and reminded them of his care for their welfare. The army leaders then repented and asked for mercy. The following excerpt is Arrian's recounting of the scene.

THE LIFE OF ALEXANDER THE GREAT

Alexander, the moment he heard of this change of heart, hastened out to meet them, and he was so touched by their groveling repentance and their bitter lamentations that the tears came into his eyes. While they continued to beg for his pity, he stepped forward as if to speak, but was anticipated by one Callines, an officer.... distinguished by both age and rank. "My lord," he cried, "what hurts us is that you have made Persians your kinsmen- Persians are called "Alexander's kinsmen"- Persians kiss you. But no Macedonian has yet had a taste of this honor."

"Every man of you," Alexander replied, "I regard as my kinsman, and from now on that is what I shall call you.

Thereupon Callines came up to him and kissed him, and all the others who wished to do so kissed him too. Then they picked up their weapons and returned to their quarters singing the song of victory at the top of their voices.

To mark the restoration of harmony, Alexander offered sacrifice to the gods he was accustomed to honor, and gave a public banquet which he himself attended, sitting among the Macedonians, all of whom were present. Next to them the Persians had their places, and next to the Persians, distinguished foreigners of other nations; Alexander and his friends dipped their wine from the same bowl and poured the same libations.... The chief object of his prayers was that Persians and Macedonians might rule together in harmony as an imperial power. It is said that 9,000 people attended the banquet; they unanimously drank the same toast, and followed it by the song of victory.

After this all the Macedonians- about 10,000 all told- who were too old for service or in any way unfit, got their discharge at their own request.

TEXTUAL QUESTIONS FOR ANALYSIS

1. From the evidence of the source, what were the grievances of the Macedonians? Why was Alexander apparently not aware of the problem?
2. What type of leadership qualities did Alexander show in dealing with the problem? What type of reaction did he apparently expect when he made his announcement?
3. Was Alexander's concept of international cooperation advanced for his day? How did he attempt to show special favor to the Macedonians at the banquet?
4. Why would an Egyptian pharaoh not have had to deal with a problem like this in his army?

Source: E. Iliff Rolbson, trans., *Arrian* (Cambridge: Harvard University Press, 1933), Vol. 2, pp. 225-229.

CHAPTER 11
THE ROMAN REPUBLIC

Roman society in the early days of the Republic was divided rather clearly into the ruling patrician class and the subject plebeians. The law code below, known as the Twelve Tables of Roman law, was first promulgated in the mid-fifth century B.C.E. at the insistence of the plebeians, as a way to provide them with some legal security against the economic and political power of the patricians. The Twelve Tables refers to the fact that the laws were supposedly at first written upon twelve stone tablets. All later Roman law would be considered to be based, at least in part, upon the Twelve Tables, and Roman orators of the later Republic and the Empire would invoke the Twelve Tables as justification for policies and actions, much like modern American politicians invoke the Declaration of Independence and the Constitution. The Twelve Tables provides us a good view of the economic, social, and political world of the early Republic. They reveal to us a predominantly agricultural and pastoral society attempting to codify existing customs into statutory law. The law code is notable for its formality, its harsh standards, and its secular character. The Romans attempted to separate religious and civil law in this code, a unique achievement for the ancient world.

THE TWELVE TABLES OF ROMAN LAW

Table I

If a plaintiff summons a defendant to court, he shall go. If he does not go, the plaintiff shall call the witness thereto. Then only shall he take the defendant by force.
If a defendant shirks or takes to his heels, the plaintiff shall lay hands on him.
For a landowner, a landowner shall be surety; but for a commoner, let any one willing be his protector....

Table IV

A father shall quickly kill.... a dreadfully deformed child.
If a father three times surrenders a son for sale, the son shall be free from the father.
A child born ten months after the father's death will not be admitted into a legal inheritance.

Table V

Females shall remain in guardianship to their fathers or husbands even when they have attained their majority....
According as a person shall will regarding his household, chattels, or guardianship of his estate, this shall be binding.
If a person dies intestate (without a will), and has no self-successor, the nearest kinsman shall have possession of the deceased's household.

Table VIII

If any person has sung or composed against another person a song such as was causing slander or insult to another, he shall be clubbed to death.

If a person has maimed another's limb, let there be retaliation in kind unless he makes agreement for a settlement with him....

For pasturing on, or cutting secretly by night, another's crops acquired by tillage, there shall be capital punishment in the case of an adult malefactor.... In the case of a person under the age of puberty, ... he shall be scourged or settlement shall be made for the harm done by paying double damages.

Any person who destroys by burning any building or crops deposited alongside a house shall be bound, scourged, and put to death.... provided that he has committed the said misdeed with malice aforethought; but if he shall have committed it by accident, ... it is ordained that he repair the damage....

If theft has been done by night, if the owner kills the thief, the thief shall be held lawfully killed.

It is forbidden that a thief be killed by day.... unless he defends himself with a weapon...

A person who has been found guilty of giving false witness shall be hurled down to their death from the Tarpeian Rock.

Table IX
The penalty shall be capital punishment for a judge.... who has been found guilty of receiving a bribe for giving a decision.

The putting to death.... of any man who has not been convicted, whosoever he might be (patrician or plebeian), is forbidden.

TEXTUAL QUESTIONS FOR ANALYSIS

1. Compare this law code to Hammurabi's Code of Chapter 2. Although the Roman patricians obviously enjoyed some special status, is this code as class based as that of Hammurabi's? Is there any major difference in the status of women?
2. What type of power did a Roman husband and father have over his family?
3. Why do you think the law code provides such harsh punishment for the destruction or theft of crops?
4. Explain why you think the law provides different penalties for theft by day and night. Why do you think such harsh penalties are provided for lying under oath and corrupt judges?

Source: N. Lewis and M. Reinhold, eds. and trans., *Roman Civilization, Sourcebook I, The Republic* (New York: Columbia University Press, 1966), pp. 102-109.

CHAPTER 12
THE ROMAN EMPIRE

The great achievement of Augustus was to bring peace and order to Roman society after a period of civil war and social upheaval. But this peace and order were brought about by ending the Republic and maintaining its institutions as a cover for his personal authority. The period of the Pax Romana which he began would be a period of peace and prosperity for most citizens of the Empire, but there were regrets by many of the old patrician order who saw the new system as a symbol of the moral decline of the new age. One of these sentimental republicans was Tacitus, considered by many scholars to be one of the best Roman historians, who wrote his ANNALS in about 120 C.E. In the following selection from this monumental work, Tacitus looks back about 100 years to the period when Augustus made himself the first Roman emperor, in fact, if not in name. He is attempting to explain how it was done, and why the system was still going strong after 100 years. It is surprisingly modern in tone, and expresses very well the aristocratic patrician view that the empire may be peaceful, but it has lost the old republican virtues of self-government, public morality, and private modesty.

THE ANNALS OF TACITUS

When the last army of the Republic had fallen with Brutus and Cassius on the field; when Sextus Pompeius had been crushed in Sicily; and when the deposition of Lepidus, followed by the death of Antonius, had left Augustus sole leader of the Julian party, he laid aside the title of Triumvir (Augustus had been one of three leaders), assumed the Consulship, and professed himself content with the Tribunitian Power for the protection of the plebs. But when he had won the soldiery by bounties, the populace by cheap food, and all classes alike by the sweets of peace, he rose higher and higher by degrees, and drew into his own hands all the functions of the Senate, the magistrates and the laws. And there was no one to oppose; for the most ardent patriots had fallen on the field, or in the proscriptions; and the rest of the nobles, advanced in wealth and place in proportion to their servility, and drawing profits out of the new order of affairs, preferred the security of the present to the hazards of the past.

Nor did the provinces resent the change; for the rule of the Senate and the People had become odious to them from the contests between great leaders, and the greed of magistrates, against whom the law, upset by force, by favor, and, in truth, by bribery, were powerless to protect them....

Thus a revolution had been accomplished. The old order had passed away; everything had suffered change. The days of equality were gone: men looked to the Prince for his commands, having no anxiety for the present, so long as Augustus was not too old, and had the strength, to keep himself, his house and the public peace secure. But when he advanced in years, when his health and strength failed, and his approaching end gave birth to new hopes, some few discoursed idly on the blessings of liberty; many dreaded war; some longed for it.

TEXTUAL QUESTIONS FOR ANALYSIS

1. Describe in your own words how Augustus was able to win the approval of the army and the common people. According to Tacitus, why was there no effective opposition?
2. When Tacitus speaks of the provinces, he is referring to the empire outside of Italy. Why did the various parts of the empire welcome the rule of Augustus?
3. Remembering that Tacitus was an aristocrat, what does he mean when he says that the "days of equality were gone."
4. What are the dangers of one-man rule that Tacitus outlines in the last paragraph? Have these dangers changed in the political world of today?

Source: G. G. Ramsey, trans., *The Annals of Tacitus* (London: John Murray, 1904), pp. 3-5 and p. 8.

CHAPTER 13
ORDINARY LIVES IN THE CLASSICAL AGE

Due to the spread of literacy, and the ease of writing in the alphabetic systems of Greek and Latin, scholars have much more information about the daily lives of even common people from the Classical Age than is true of earlier periods. The following is a marriage contract from 92 B.C.E. in the Egypt of the Ptolemies. It is an agreement between two Persians living in Egypt, an indication of the cosmopolitan nature of the Hellenistic world. The Greek influence on that world is also evident in that although the bride and groom identify themselves as Persian, their names are Greek. They may very well have been descendants of those Greeks who chose to live in Persia after its conquest by Alexander the Great. The significance of this papyrus scroll for modern historians is the light that it throws upon marriage, a fundamental social institution for the Hellenistic age as much as for our own. Much of the contract revolves around the dowry, the property brought by the wife from her family into the marriage, and the rights and obligations of the husband and wife toward each other. From a modern perspective, the most surprising aspect is the degree of protection provided to the wife. Greek conceptions of property rights and the necessity of written contracts obviously had penetrated deeply into the social system of the Hellenistic world.

MARRIAGE CONTRACT

In the 22nd year of the reign of Ptolemy also called Alexander, the god Philometor, the priest of Alexander and the other priests being as written in Alexandria, the 11th of the month Xandicus, which is the 11th of Mecheir, at Kerkeosiris in the division of Polemon of the Arsinoite nome, Philiscus son of Apollonius, a Persian, acknowledges to Apollonia, ...daughter of Heraclides, a Persian, having with her as guardian her brother Apollonius, that he has received from her in copper money 2 talents 4000 drachmae, the dowry for herself, Apollonia, agreed upon with him. Apollonia shall live with Philiscus, obeying him as a wife should her husband, owning their property in common with him. All necessaries and clothing and whatever else is proper for a wedded wife Philiscus shall supply to Apollonia, whether he is at home or abroad, in proportion to their means. It shall not be lawful for Philiscus to bring in another wife besides Apollonia, nor to keep a concubine or boy, nor to have children by another woman while Apollonia lives, nor to inhabit another house over which Apollonia is not mistress, nor to eject or insult or ill-treat her, nor to alienate any of their property to the detriment of Apollonia. If he is proved to be doing any of these things or fails to supply her with necessaries or clothing or other things as stated, Philiscus shall forthwith forfeit to Apollonia the dowry of 2 talents 4000 drachmae of copper. In like manner it shall not be lawful for Apollonia to spend the night or day away from the house of Philiscus without the consent of Philiscus or to consort with another man or to dishonor the common home or to cause Philiscus to be shamed by any act that brings shame upon a husband. If Apollonia chooses of her own will to separate from Philiscus, Philiscus shall repay her the bare dowry within ten days from the date of the demand. If he does not repay as stated, he shall forthwith forfeit to her one and a half times the amount of the dowry received.

Witnesses: Dionysius son of Patron, Dionysius son of Hermaiscus, Theon son of Ptolemaeus, Didymus son of Ptolemaeus, Dionysius son of Dionysius, Heraclius son of Diocles, all six Macedonians.... Dionysius son of Hermaiscus, the aforesaid, wrote for Philiscus, as he is illiterate. I, Dionysius, have received the contract, being valid. Deposited for registration on Mecheir 11 of year 22....

TEXTUAL QUESTIONS FOR ANALYSIS

1. It is hard to be precise about the value of the amount mentioned here, but the talent was a large unit of monetary value in the Hellenistic world. Since the husband is required to return the dowry if the marriage fails, what is he expected to do with it?
2. What are the differences between the obligations of husband and wife?
3. Who may end the marriage and for what reasons? What rights does Apollonia have if she breaks her part of the contract?
4. What are similarities and differences between this contract and modern marriage vows?

Source: A. S. Hunt and C. C. Edgar, trans., *Papyri: Volume I, Non-Literary Papyri: Private Documents* (Cambridge: Harvard University Press, 1932), pp. 24-26.

CHAPTER 14
ROME'S TRANSFORMATION AND THE BEGINNINGS OF EUROPE

The rise, spread, and eventual triumph of Christianity as the official state religion of the late Roman Empire is one of the great stories of the ancient world. But the Christianity of the Roman empire was not the Christianity of the modern western world. There were differences of doctrine among various groups, and residual paganism still flourished, especially in the rural areas among the peasantry. Thus, toleration of different views and other religions was not an acceptable option to the early Christian emperors and Church fathers. They viewed their faith and views as the only correct version of religious truth, and toleration of other views was considered sinful, and a sign of weakness.

From Constantine forward, all Roman emperors were Christian, and the Church greatly benefited from this imperial patronage. Christianity was a minority religion of the empire at the beginning of the fourth century when Constantine gave it legal toleration, but by the time Theodosius assumed the throne in 379 C.E., the faith had enjoyed over 60 years of official favor, and Christians were by then the majority in many urban areas. Emperor Theodosius issued a series of imperial edicts between 380 and his death in 395 that made Christianity the official state religion, banned other religions, except for the Jews, and extended official benefits and protections to Christian clergy and churches. The following selections are from the THEODOSIAN CODE, a collection of imperial laws published under Emperor Theodosius II in 438 C.E. They provide us with an official legal view of the first century of imperial Christianity as Theodosius I and his successors sought to eliminate any opposition to the new state religion.

THE THEODOSIAN CODE

The Imperial Church- February 28, 380

All peoples, whom the moderation of our Clemency rules, we wish to be engaged in that religion, which the divine Peter, the apostle, is declared.... to have transmitted to the Romans and which, it is clear the pontiff Damascus and Peter, bishop of Alexandria, a man of apostolic sanctity, follow: that is, that according to apostolic discipline and evangelic doctrine we should believe the sole Deity of the Father and of the Son and of the Holy Spirit under an equal Majesty and under a pious Trinity.

We order those following this law to assume the name of Catholic (universal) Christians, but the rest, since we judge them demented and insane, to sustain the infamy of heretical dogma and their meeting places to take the name of churches, to be smitten first by divine vengeance, then also by the punishment of our authority, which we have claimed in accordance with the celestial will.

Heretics- May 11, 391

Those who shall have betrayed the holy faith and shall have profaned holy baptism should be segregated from all persons' association, should be debarred from testifying, should not have the right of making a will, should succeed to no one in an inheritance, should be written by no one as heirs.

And these also we should have commanded to be banished to a distance and to be removed far away, if it had not seemed to be a greater penalty for them to dwell among men and to lack men's approbation.

But they never shall return to their previous status, the shame of their conduct shall not be obliterated by penitence and shall not be concealed by any shade of elaborate defense or protection, since things which are fabricated and fashioned cannot protect those who have polluted the faith which they vowed to God, and who, betraying the divine mystery (baptism), have turned to profanations. And indeed for the lapsed and the errant there is help, but for the lost—the profaners of holy baptism—there is no aid through any remedy of penitence, which is to be available for other crimes.

Heretics- May 19, 391

We order the heretics polluted contagions to be driven from cities, to be ejected from villages, and the communities not at all to be available for any meetings, lest in any place a sacrilegious company of such persons should be collected. Neither public meeting places for their perversity nor more hidden retreats for their errors should be granted.

Pagans- August 7, 395

We ordain that none may have the liberty of approaching any (i.e., pagan) shrine or temple whatever or of performing abominable sacrifices at any place or time whatever.

Jews- August 6, 412

No one, on the ground that he is a Jew, when he is innocent, should be condemned....

Their synagogues or habitations should not be burned... nor should not be damaged wrongfully without any reason...

But as we desire this to be provided for the persons of the Jews, so we decree also that the following warning ought to be made: that Jews perchance should not become insolent and, elated by their own security, should not commit anything rash against reverence for the Christian worship.

The Clergy- October 21, 319

Whoever devote to divine worship the services of religion, that is, those who are called clergymen, should be excused entirely from all public services, lest through certain persons' sacrilegious malice they should be diverted from divine services.

TEXTUAL QUESTIONS FOR ANALYSIS

1. Heretics are singled out for much more severe treatment than either pagans or those who once believed, but have since fallen away from the true faith. Why?
2. What specific types of economic and social punishment are outlined for heretics that would make it difficult for any person of property or status to continue being a heretic?
3. Why do you think the code provides basic protection for Jews, rather than banning the religion?
4. What tangible benefits would the empire derive from its special treatment of the clergy?
5. How does the underlying attitude here differ from the concept of religious enlightenment found in Hinduism and Buddhism?

Source: Clyde Pharr, trans., *The Theodosian Code and Novels and the Sirmondian Constitutions* (Princeton: Princeton University Press, 1952), pp. 17, 115, 119.

CHAPTER 15
ISLAM

While the Qur'an is considered by devout Muslims to be the direct revelations of God to Muhammad, and is thus the most sacred scripture of Islam, the HADITH or tales of tradition constitute a much larger and very important body of scripture as well. The Qur'an was put in its final form within less than fifty years after Muhammad's death, but it was not until about 200 years later that Islamic scholars began to collect and organize systematically the various stories and traditions that circulated about the Prophet and his first followers. These early collections were quite lengthy, one of the most famous containing over 7,000 tales. The Hadith were used by Islamic scholars as a way of teaching moral lessons based on the life of Prophet. They provided a human side to the life and teachings of Muhammad, and dealt with everyday issues of the community of the faithful. Each story deals with something the Prophet said or did, or something that was said or done in his presence, and thus approved by him. Unlike the Qur'an there has never been a single source of Hadith, but some are considered more authentic than others. Most Muslims today believe that a true hadith contains the original tradition of the first Islamic community and the teachings of Muhammad, and thereby provides a perfect model for behavior in most aspects of life. The following selection is from a collection of hadith called THE GARDENS OF THE RIGHTEOUS, compiled in the 13th century by the famous Syrian Islamic scholar Imam Nawawi. This collection is considered authentic because he tied each story to a passage in the Qur'an and stipulated the source of the story from the companions of the Prophet.

THE HADITH OF IMAM NAWAWI- THE GARDENS OF THE RIGHTEOUS

On the Superiority of the Poor and Weak among Moslems

Allah, the Exalted, has said: Continue thy companionship with those who call on their Lord, morning and evening, seeking His pleasure, and look not beyond them.(18.29)

Haritha ibn Wahb relates that he heard the Honorable Prophet say: Shall I tell you who are the dwellers of Paradise? It is every weak one who is accounted weak and is looked down upon, who if he takes an oath relying upon Allah He would fulfill it. Now shall I tell you who are the denizens of the Fire? It is every ignorant, impertinent, prideful, and arrogant one....

Usamah relates that the Honorable Prophet said: I stood at the gate of Paradise and observed that the generality of those who entered it were the lowly. The wealthy had been held back from it. Then those condemned to the Fire were ordered to it and I stood at the gate of the Fire and observed that the generality of those who entered it were women.

On Kind Treatment of Orphans, the Weak, the Poor, and the Lowly

Allah, the Exalted, has said: Continue to be kindly gracious towards the believers(15.89). Continue thy companionship with those who call on their Lord, morning and evening, seeking His pleasure, and look not beyond them, for if thou dost that thou wouldst be seeking the values of this life(18.29).

Oppress not the orphan and chide not him who asks(93-10-11).
Knowest thou him who rejects the faith? That is the one who drives sway the orphan and urges not the feeding of the poor(107.2-4).

Abu Hurairah relates that the Honorable Prophet said: He who exerts himself on behalf of widows and the indigent is like one who strives in the cause of Allah; and the narrator thinks he added: and like the guardian who never retreats, and like one who observes the fast and does not break it....

Anas relates that the Honorable Prophet said: He who brings up two girls through their childhood will appear on the Day of Judgment attached to me like two fingers of a hand....

Ayesha (one of Muhammed's wives) relates: A poor woman came to me with her two daughters. I gave her three dates. She gave one to each girl and raised the third to her own mouth to eat. The girls asked her for it. So she broke it into two parts and gave one to each of the girls. I was much struck by her action and mentioned what she had done to the Honorable Prophet. He said: Allah appointed Paradise for her in consequence of it....

Abu Shuraih Khuwailad ibn Amr Khuza'i relates that the Honorable Prophet said: Allah, I declare sinful any failure to safeguard the rights of two weak ones; orphans and women.

On a Husband's Right Concerning His Wife

Allah, the Exalted, has said: Men are appointed guardians over women, because of that in respect of which Allah has made some of them excel others, and because the men spend their wealth. So virtuous women are obedient and safeguard, with Allah's help, matters the knowledge of which is shared by them with their husbands(4.35)....

Ibn Umar relates that the Honorable Prophet said: Every one of you is a steward and is accountable for that which is committed to his charge. The ruler is a steward and is accountable for his charge, a man is a steward in respect of his household, a woman is a steward in respect of her husband's house and his children. Thus every one of you is a steward and is accountable for that which is committed to his charge.

Abu Ali Talq ibn Ali relates that the Honorable Prophet said: When a man calls his wife for his need, she should go to him even if she is occupied in baking bread.

Usamah ibn Zaid relates that the Honorable Prophet said: I am not leaving a more harmful trial for man than woman.

TEXTUAL QUESTIONS FOR ANALYSIS

1. How do these hadith relate to Islamic doctrine as discussed in your text?
2. How does the male domination found here compare with male domination found in other civilizations you have studied?
3. Based on what you have read about Muhammad, what might be the basis for the emphasis on the kind treatment for the poor, orphans, and widows?
4. Compared to the Qur'an, what is the overall tone of these hadith, and how could they used in the teaching of morality?

Source: Muhammad Zafrulla Khan, trans., *The Gardens of the Righteous* (London: Curzon Press, 1975), pp. 60-63, 68-69.

CHAPTER 16
MATURE ISLAMIC SOCIETY AND INSTITUTIONS

The Abbasid dynasty that ruled in Baghdad from the mid- 8th century to the mid-13th century represented the height of Islamic culture and achievement. At a time when western Europe was largely rural, illiterate, and economically backward, the Abbasid Caliphates ruled over an empire that stretched from the Indus River to the shores of the Atlantic. Baghdad was constructed by the second Abbasid Caliphate, al-Mansur (754-775), in only four years to serve as a new capital city for the Islamic empire. It was built as a circular fortress, surrounded by huge brick walls, with the great palace of the Caliph located in the very center of the city and protected by a ninety-foot wall and deep moat. Drawn by its ideal location for trade, and the presence of the government, merchants soon flocked to the city, and within twenty years, its population is estimated by modern scholars as close to a million, at a time when Paris and London both had populations of about twenty thousand.

The following selection was written by an anonymous Persian nobleman to his father in the late eighth century, during the reign of Haroun al-Rashid (786-809), considered by many scholars to be the most capable of the Abbasid caliphs. As you read the selection, remember that the city being described by the young Persian, probably a student at the university established by al-Mansur, was only about fifty years old.

THE BAGHDAD OF HAROUN AL-RASHID

When I wandered about in the city after a long absence, I found it in an expansion of prosperity that I had not observed before this time. The resplendent buildings that rose in the city ... were not sufficient for its wealthy people until they extended to the houses of the eastern quarter know as Rusafa. They built high castles and ornamented houses in this quarter, and set up markets, mosques, and public baths. The attention of al-Rashid.... was directed toward adorning it with public buildings, until the old Baghdad became like an ancient town whose beauties were assembled in a section of the city which was created near by it.

I admired the arrival of buildings in Baghdad because of the overcrowdedness of the people I had seen in its sections. Their billowing is like the sea in its expanses; their number is said to exceed 1,500,000, and no other city in the world has such a sum or even half its amount....

It is difficult for me, with this pen which is of limited substance, to describe the glorious qualities of the city which are but a small part of the honor it achieves, such that it prides itself in the splendor of power. ...The people of wealth walk with slave boys and retinue whose number the listener will fancy to be far from the truth. I witnessed at Attabiyya station a prince who was riding with a hundred horsemen and was surrounded by slave boys, even filling the road and blocking the path of the people until they passed.... Nor was any Caliph ever known to be more generous than he (Haroun al-Rashid) in the handing out of wealth. It is said that he spends ten thousand dirhams (a silver coin) every day for his food, and perhaps the cooks would prepare for him thirty kinds of food. Abu Yusuf informed me that when the Caliph consummated his marriage to Zubaida, the daughter of Ja'far the Barmakid, he gave a banquet unprecedented in Islam. He gave away unlimited presents at this banquet, even giving containers of gold filled with silver, containers of silver filled with gold, bags of musk, and pieces of ambergris. The total expenditure on this banquet reached 55,000,000 dirhams. The Caliph commanded that Zubaida be presented in a gown of pearls whose price no one was able to appraise. He adorned her with pieces of jewelry, so much so that she was not able to walk because of the great number of jewels which were upon her. This example of extravagance had no precedent among the kings of Persia, the emperors of Byzantium, or the princes of the Umayyads, despite the great amounts of money which they had at their disposal....

Affluence is abundant among the upper rank of those who are masters of the state. It then diminishes little by little among those of lesser rank, until only a small amount remains for the general public. As for those who do not enjoy the exalted power and breadth of bounty of the kings, they begin to equip themselves with all the good things after they have gone on journeys which gain them experience, show them wondrous things, and give them profits. The people in the provinces come to them with the grandest of all the types of their wares, until markets have become plentiful in Baghdad. They have advanced from requesting necessities to the acquisition of things for beautification and decoration. This may be seen in the case of their purchase of arms inlaid with gold, their competing in costly jewels, ornamented vessels, and splendid furniture, and their acquisition of a large number of slave boys, female singers, and those things which they send out their retainers to seek in the provinces. When every expensive and rare thing in the country was brought to them, I realized that the beauties of the world had been assembled in Baghdad....

TEXTUAL QUESTIONS FOR ANALYSIS

1. From the evidence of the source, what is one of the main business activities of Baghdad?
2. Based on your reading in the text, what was the source of the great wealth of the Abbasids as described in this letter. Why was Baghdad a much larger and wealthier city than any city in Western Europe at this time?
3. According to the letter, how was the wealth of the city distributed among the various classes? How pervasive does slavery appear to be?
4. Assuming you could not be a member of the ruling class, what occupation would you

choose if you could travel back to ancient Baghdad, and why?

Source: Ilse Lichtenstadter, ed., *Introduction to Classical Arabic Literature* (New York: Twayne Publishers Inc., 1974), pp. 357-360.

CHAPTER 17
INDIAN CIVILIZATION IN ITS GOLDEN AGE

During the period of the Gupta dynasty (320-480 C.E.), a new devotional type of Hinduism emerged, and has remained to the present day one of the most popular forms of worship in the ancient religion. The Way of Devotion, or bhakti in Sanskrit, is the concentration of the worshipper upon one of the three divine personalities of Brahman, the One- Brahma the Creator, Vishnu the Preserver, or Shiva the Destroyer. Of these, Brahma was the least widely worshipped, being perceived as a remote creator who did not concern himself with worldly affairs. Vishnu and Shiva, however, became the focus of widespread devotion. Worshippers did not deny the reality of the many other aspects of divinity, or the other gods of the Hindu pantheon; they chose Shiva or Vishnu because each represented a special part of the totality of Divine Reality. Those who worshipped Vishnu believed that he had assumed human form on a number of occasions in order to teach and bless humanity. These personifications were called avatars, and the most well known and widely revered were the warriors Rama and Krishna. The object of the Way of Devotion was to offer such a god exclusive and total devotion in the hope of sharing in the perfection of the god and thus achieving rebirth at a higher level in the next cycle of rebirth. The BAGHAVAD GITA was the most widely read Hindu scripture of this period, and has remained so today. But during the Gupta era a new There were eighteen major Puranas composed over a period of several hundred years. These stories were intended for the people, not the Brahmin priests, and their long rambling narratives always ended with the same basic message- a particular god, Brahma, Vishnu, or Shiva, deserved unreserved worship from his followers, for which the devotee would receive blessings in both this life and the next. Bhakti became the overwhelming form of Hinduism for the lower castes, and helped Hinduism meet and eventually overcome the spread of Buddhism in India. The following selection comes from the closing section of the VISHNU PURANA, one of the most popular of these devotional stories, composed about 500 C.E.

THE VISHNU PURANA

I have related to you this Purana, which is equal to the Vedas in sanctity, and by hearing which all faults and sins whatever are expiated.... By hearing this, all sins are at once obliterated. In this also the glorious Vishnu has been revealed, the cause of creation, preservation, and destruction of the world; the soul of all things, and himself all things: by the repetition of whose name man is undoubtedly liberated from all sins, which fly like wolves that are frightened by a lion. The repetition of his name with devout faith is the best remover of all sins, destroying them as fire purifies the metal from the dross.... He who is all that is.... he who is all things, who knows all things, who is the form of all things, being without form himself, and of whom whatever is.... all consists- he, the glorious Vishnu, the destroyer of all sin- is described in this Purana. By hearing this Purana an equal recompense is obtained to that which is derived from.... fasting at the holy places.... This Purana is the best of all preservatives for those who are afraid of worldly existence, a certain alleviation of the sufferings of men, and remover of all imperfections.... Whoever hears this great mystery.... shall be freed from all his sins. He who hears this every day acquits himself of his daily obligations to ancestors, gods, and men....

I adore him, that first of gods, Vishnu, who is without end and without beginning, without growth, without decay, without death; who is substance that knows not change. I adore that ever inexhaustible spirit, who assumed human form; who, though one, became many; who, though pure, became impure, by appearing in many and various shapes; who is endowed with divine wisdom, and is the author of the preservation of all creatures. I adore him, who is the one conjoined essence and object of both meditative wisdom and active virtue; who is watchful in providing for human enjoyments; who is one with the three qualities; who, without undergoing change, is the cause of the evolution of the world; who exists of his own essence, ever exempt from decay.... May that unborn, eternal Vishnu, whose form is manifold, and whose essence is composed of both nature and spirit, bestow upon all mankind that blessed state which knows neither birth nor decay!

TEXTUAL QUESTIONS FOR ANALYSIS

1. Can you detect any similarities between the Hindu Way of Devotion or bhakti, and Christian ideas of the nature of God and worship?
2. From the above selection, list ten of the qualities of Vishnu. How are all of the qualities similar?
3. Why do you think this form of Hinduism proved to be quite popular with the lower castes?
4. In this passage, what is the power of the name of Vishnu, and what is the most important requirement for his followers?

Source: H. W. Wilson, trans., *The Vishnu Purana*, 3rd ed. (Calcutta: Punthi Pustak, 1961), pp. 516-520.

CHAPTER 18
CHINA TO THE MONGOL CONQUEST

Study of the Confucian classics became the most important avenue to political and social power for ambitious young men in China during the Han dynasty. However, Confucianism did not accord women equal status to men because women were considered incapable and unworthy of a literary education. Women were scarcely mentioned in the Confucian classics, a clear indication of their relatively low status in the Chinese value system. This subservience of women to men was taken as the natural order of things by most Confucian scholars, and the maintenance of a proper relationship between men and women was considered essential for insuring social harmony, the most important objective of Confucianism.

But women were accorded considerable status and honor in traditional Chinese society and Confucian doctrine in their roles as mothers and mothers-in-law, and within those positions women could and did exercise substantial power within the family structure. Moreover, there are several examples within the period covered by this chapter of exceptional women who managed to acquire literary educations and rise above their preordained stations to positions of influence and prestige. The most famous female Confucian of the Han dynasty was Ban Zhao (45-116 C.E.), the daughter of the widely respected writer and government administrator, Ban Biao. She received her basic education from her literate mother, and married at the age of fourteen. She was widowed while still a young mother, and never remarried, devoting herself to writing and scholarship, eventually acquiring such renown that she was brought to the imperial court to be the tutor and adviser of the Empress. Her younger brother was the official court historian, and upon his unexpected death, she completed his history of the dynasty, entitled the HAN ANNALS. Her success at this led to her appointment as the official court historian under the Emperor Han Hedi (88-105 C.E.). Later in life she composed her most famous work, LESSONS FOR WOMEN, which was intended to be an instructional manual on proper behavior and virtue for young women. Since traditional Confucian texts contained very little specific information or guidelines for a woman's daily life, she sought to provide a practical set of rules that would enable all women, and especially young women, to insure harmony within the home. Her book became a classic, and for centuries the work of this female Confucian was used as an authoritative guide for young brides in China as they sought to establish domestic tranquility.

LESSONS FOR WOMEN

HUMILITY- ...Let a woman modestly yield to others; let her respect others; let her put others first, herself last. Should she do good, let her not mention it; should she do something bad, let her not deny it. Let her bear disgrace; let her even endure when others speak or do evil to her. Always let her seem to tremble and to fear. When a woman follows such maxims as these, then she may be said to humble herself before others.

Let a woman retire late to bed, but rise early to duties; let her not dread tasks by day or night. Let her not refuse to perform domestic duties whether easy or difficult. That which must be done, let her finish completely, tidily, and systematically. When a woman follows such rules as these, then she may be said to be industrious.

Let a woman be correct in manner and upright in character in order to serve her husband. Let her live in purity and quietness of spirit, and attend to her own affairs. Let her love not gossip and silly laughter. Let her cleanse and purify and arrange in order the wine and the food for the offerings to the ancestors. When a woman observes such principles as these, then she may be said to continue ancestral worship.

No woman who observes these three fundamentals of life has ever had a bad reputation or has fallen into disgrace. If a woman fails to observe them, how can her name be honored; how can she but bring disgrace upon herself?

HUSBAND AND WIFE- If a husband be unworthy then he possesses nothing by which to control his wife. If a wife be unworthy, then she possesses nothing with which to serve her husband. If a husband does not control his wife, then the rules of conduct manifesting his authority are abandoned and broken. If a wife does not serve her husband, then the proper relationship between men and women and the natural order of things are neglected and destroyed. As a matter of fact the purpose of these two, the controlling of women by men, and the serving of men by women, is the same....

WOMANLY QUALIFICATIONS- A woman ought to have four qualifications: (1) womanly virtue; (2) womanly words; (3) womanly bearing; and (4) womanly work....

To guard carefully her chastity; to control circumspectly her behavior; in every motion to exhibit modesty; and to model each act on the best usage, this is womanly virtue.

To choose her words with care; to avoid vulgar language; to speak at appropriate times; and not to weary others with much conversation, may be called the characteristics of womanly words.

To wash and scrub filth away; to keep clothes and ornaments fresh and clean; to wash the head and bathe the body regularly, and to keep the person free from disgraceful filth, may be called the characteristics of womanly bearing.

With whole-hearted devotion to sew and to weave; to love not gossip and silly laughter; in cleanliness and order to prepare the wine and food for serving guests, may be called the characteristics of womanly work.
These four qualifications characterize the greatest virtue of a woman. No woman can afford to be without them. In fact they are very easy to possess if a woman only treasure them in her heart....

TEXTUAL QUESTIONS FOR ANALYSIS

1. How did Ban Zhao's life obviously differ from that of most Chinese women of her day?
2. What would be her advice to a young woman who wished to pursue a career of her own, as well as marriage and family? Why?
3. Within marriage, how did she depict the ideal husband and wife?
6. What could be considered the positive and negative aspects of her advice? Have you encountered in your text any other civilizations that had similar views on women? Why would modern Westerners consider her advice out-dated? Are there any societies today that would consider the above selection correct advice for young women?

Source: Lynn H. Nelson and Patrick Peebles, eds., *Classics of Eastern Thought* (New York: Harcourt Brace Jovanovich, 1991), pp. 101-105.

CHAPTER 19
JAPAN AND SOUTHEAST ASIA

As your text points out, the dominant theme of early Japanese history is cultural borrowing from China and Korea. But the Japanese modified the Confucianism, Buddhism, written language, and governmental systems that they borrowed to suit their island nation and their own cultural inclinations. Perhaps because they did import so much of their civilization, one the central themes of early Japanese culture is the teaching of Japan's uniqueness. Thus, in their creation myth, the Sun Goddess, Amaterasu Omikami, is depicted as creating the home islands of Japan and the human population of these islands before creating anything or anyone else. By the fourteenth century, Japan had developed along different lines from that of China and Korea. Its government was a feudal system, dominated by a powerful nobility, with a figurehead emperor who was regarded as descended from the Sun Goddess. Its language was quite different from the parent Chinese script, and in religion Zen Buddhism had become a Japanese addition to the ancient faith. The Japanese had also survived and defeated the determined attack by the Chinese Mongol dynasty to add them to the Chinese empire in 1281, saved by samurai bravery and the kamikaze, or divine wind, that destroyed the invasion fleet. It was in this atmosphere of cultural nationalism that the following selection was composed. THE RECORDS OF THE LEGITIMATE SUCCESSION OF THE DIVINE SOVEREIGNS was composed in the early fourteenth century by Kitabatake Chikafusa, an official court historian, and represents an attempt to establish the cultural uniqueness and superiority of Japan. In this chronicle, Chikafusa presents a Japan that is not a borrower, but an inventor of the culture and civilization of other nations. Confucianism and Buddhism are presented as later developments from the native Japanese Shintoism, and Japan is presented as the superior society relative to China. One of the most important proofs of this is the notion that all Japanese emperors have come from the same lineage, which was clearly not true of China. A realm with an unbroken line of divinely ordained emperors, according to the author, is clearly to be considered superior to nations with multiple dynasties.

THE RECORDS OF THE LEGITIMATE SUCCESSION OF THE DIVINE SOVEREIGNS

Japan is the divine country. The heavenly ancestor it was who first laid its foundations, and the Sun Goddess left her descendants to reign over it forever and ever. This is true only of our country, and nothing similar may be found in foreign lands. This is why it is called the divine country....

In the Age of the Gods, Japan was known as the "ever-fruitful land of reed-covered plains and luxuriant rice fields." It is also called the country of the great eight islands. This name was given because eight islands were produced when the Male Deity and the Female Deity begot Japan. It is also called Yamato, which is the name of the central part of the eight islands.

...Japan is the Land of the Sun Goddess, or it may have thus been called because it is near the place where the sun rises....

...Since Japan is a separate continent, distinct from both India and China and lying in a great ocean, it is the country where the divine illustrious imperial line has been transmitted....

The creation of heaven and earth must everywhere have been the same, for it occurred within the same universe, but the Indian, Chinese, and Japanese traditions are each different....

In China, nothing positive is stated concerning the creation of the world even though China is a country which accords special importance to the keeping of records.... In other works they speak of heaven, earth, and man as having begun in an unformed, undivided state, much as in the accounts of our Age of the Gods....

The beginnings of Japan in some ways resemble the Indian descriptions, telling as it does of the world's creation from the seed of the heavenly gods. However, whereas in our country the succession to the throne has followed a single undeviating line since the first divine ancestor, nothing of the kind has existed in India.... China is also a country of notorious disorders. Even in ancient times, when life was simple and conduct was proper, the throne was offered to wise men, and no single lineage was established.... Some of the rulers rose from the ranks of the commoners, and there were even some of barbarian origin who usurped power....

Only in our country has the succession remained inviolate, from the beginning of heaven and earth to the present. It has been maintained within a single lineage, and even when, as inevitably has happened, the succession has been transmitted collaterally, it has returned to the true line. This is due to the ever-renewed Divine Oath, and makes Japan unlike all other countries.

TEXTUAL QUESTIONS FOR ANALYSIS

1. The author speaks of the distant past as "the Age of the Gods," and speaks of ancient times as a period when "life was simple and conduct was proper." In what ways does this show his Confucian attitudes? What do you think he would say of the Japan of today?
2. With what two societies does he compare Japan, and does he find any similarities?
3. Why does he give such importance to the unbroken line of Japanese emperors, compared to those of China?
4. List four unique attributes of Japan according to Chikafusa, and why is each important? Did this attitude of superiority and uniqueness remain important in Japan in the following centuries?

Source: Ryusaku Tsunoda, William T. Bary, and Donald Keene, eds., *Sources of Japanese Tradition* (New York: Columbia University Press, 1958), Vol. 1, pp. 131-135.

CHAPTER 20
AFRICA FROM KUSH TO 1500

Mali was the second of the great West African empires to emerge before the fifteenth century. Situated in the present countries of Mali and Niger, this great trading empire developed extensive commercial connections with the Arab cities of North Africa. North African merchants brought salt and horses south over the Sahara by camel caravan and took back gold, salt, ivory, and slaves. The Arab merchants also brought Islamic culture and religion with them, and this proved to be have a lasting influence on West Africa. Islam arrived in the region during the time of the Ghana empire, but made little impact except on the ruling class. During the thirteenth to the fifteenth centuries, the period of the dominance of Mali, Islam spread widely, and increasingly became the religion of the lower classes, as well as the governing classes. The emperors of Mali were known for their devotion to Islam, and established mosques and Islamic schools throughout the empire. Arab scholars were brought to cities such as Timbuktu to become government bureaucrats for the emperor and teachers for the Islamic schools.

Much of what we know of the West African states before the fifteenth century comes from the writings of Islamic merchants, scholars, and travelers, for the African states did not have a written language. They depended on a well-developed oral history for the recording of great events and the reigns of kings. Arab scholars were used by the rulers of Ghana, Mali, and Songhai to record the laws, edicts, and history of those states, and it is from these writings that we know great rulers such as Mansa Musa. One of the most famous of the Arab writers was Ibn Battuta, the premier world traveler of his day. Born in Algiers in 1304, he became an Islamic scholar and religious judge. For over thirty years he traveled throughout the Islamic world, from India and the borders of China, to Spain, the Middle East, and West Africa. A devout Moslem, he went on pilgrimage to Mecca four times during the course of his travels. Modern scholars estimate that he traveled at least 75,000 miles during the course of three decades. Late in life he returned to Algiers and dictated a lengthy account of his travels and his observations. The following selection is from the account of his last journey, in 1352, across the Sahara to the Kingdom of Mali, where he stayed for several months in the large city of Iwalatan (present day Walata). The extent of his travels is a clear indication of the enormous expansion of Islam by the fourteenth century. Remember as you read this selection that he was a conservative Arab Islamic scholar who was endlessly fascinated by the different customs he encountered, but obviously considered his traditions superior to those of his hosts.

IBN BATTUTA AND THE KINGDOM OF MALI

The condition of these people is strange and their manners are bizarre. As for their men, there is no sexual jealousy about them. None of them is named after his father, but each traces his genealogy from his maternal uncle. A man's inheritance is not passed to his own sons but to the sons of his sister. I have never seen such a thing in any other part of the world except among the infidels who live on the Malabar coast of India. These people are Muslims who follow exactly the prescribed laws for prayer, study the laws of Islam, and know the Koran by heart. Their women are not modest in the presence of men; despite reciting their prayers punctually, they do not veil their faces. Any male who wishes to marry one of them can do so very easily, but the women do not travel with their husbands for her family would not allow it. In this country, the women are permitted to have male friends and companions among men who are not members of her family. So too for men; they are permitted to have female companions among women who are not members of his family. It happens quite often that a man would enter his own house and find his wife with one of her own friends and would not rebuke her....

Among their good qualities we can cite the following:
1. There is a small amount of crime, for these people obey the law. Their sultan does not pardon criminals.
2. Travelers and natives alike are safe from brigands, robbers, and thieves.
3. The natives do not confiscate the property of white men (i.e. Arabs) who die in this country, even if they are very wealthy; instead they entrust it to another, respected white

man to dispose of it properly.
4. The prayers are offered punctually and with fervor. Children who neglect their prayers are beaten. If you do not come to the mosque early on a Friday you cannot find a place to pray because the crowds are so large....
5. White garments are worn on Fridays....
6. They are committed to learn by heart the sublime Koran. Children who fail to learn the Koran by heart have their feet shackled and these shackles are not removed until they memorize the Koran. On a feast day I visited a judge who had his children in chains. I said to him, "Why don't you release them?" He said, "I will not do so until they know the Koran by heart."....

Among their bad qualities we can cite the following:
1. Their female servants, slave women and small daughters appear before men completely naked, exposing their private parts. Even during the month of Ramadan (the month of fasting), military commanders broke their fast in the palace of the Sultan. Twenty or more naked servant girls served them food.
2. Nude women without veils on their faces enter the palace of the Sultan. On the twenty-seventh night of Ramadan, I saw about a hundred naked female slaves coming out of the palace of the Sultan with food. Two of the Sultan's daughters, who have large breasts, were with them and they were naked.
3. These natives put dust and ashes on their head to show their education and as a sign of respect.
4. They laugh when poets recite their verse before the Sultan.
5. Finally, they eat impure meat such as dogs and donkeys.

TEXTUAL QUESTIONS FOR ANALYSIS

1. Why do you think Ibn Battuta objected to the relative freedom of women that he found in Mali?
2. Why do you think he objected to slave girls and young girls appearing nude in public?
3. What does he consider the most important good qualities of Mali? Notice that he considers many of their good qualities to be a direct result of Islam. What aspects of their society might a Christian visitor have considered good and which ones bad?
4. Look at numbers 3, 4, and 5 of his list of bad qualities. How might his opinion be a product of his own cultural bias?

Source: J. F. P. Hopkins and N. Levtzion, eds. and trans., *Corpus of Early African Sources for West African History* (Cambridge: Cambridge University Press, 1981), pp. 284-288.

CHAPTER 21
THE AMERICAS BEFORE COLUMBUS

From about 1100 to the early 1500's the Incas developed one of the most sophisticated civilizations of the Americas. Although they never developed a written language like the Maya, they managed to create and maintain an empire that stretched for over two thousand iles along the coast of western South America from Ecuador to present day Chile. It was a highly centralized state, with an elaborate system of highways that totaled about 10,000 miles. The potato was their main food crop, along with maize, and they perfected a system of terrace farming that allowed them to grow crops literally on mountainsides. Most of our knowledge of their empire comes from the written accounts of Spanish explorers, missionaries, and soldiers who began streaming into South America in the mid-1500's. The following selection is from a major work published in the 16th century entitled THE CHRONICLE OF PERU by Pedro Cieza de Leon, a Spanish nobleman and soldier who was involved in campaigns in Ecuador and Peru between 1535-1547. Although he had a role in the destruction of the Inca Empire, he obviously admired their system of government and their culture. He wrote this account between 1547-1550, and based much of his information on first-hand accounts from the Incas themselves. Today his work is considered one of the most authoritative accounts available of the Inca civilization, a civilization that was already disappearing at the time he wrote his chronicle.

THE CHRONICLE OF PERU: THE INCAS

It should be well understood that great prudence was needed to enable these kings to govern such large provinces, extending over so vast a region, parts of it rugged and covered with forests, parts mountainous, with snowy peaks and ridges, parts consisting of deserts of sand, dry and without trees or water. These regions were inhabited by many different nations, with varying languages, laws, religions, and the kings had to maintain tranquility and to rule so that all should live in peace and in friendship towards their lord. Although the city of Cuzco was the head of the empire, ... yet at certain points, as we shall also explain, the king stationed his delegates and governors, who were the most learned, the ablest, and the bravest men that could be found, and none was so youthful that he was not already in the last third part of his age. As they were faithful and none betrayed their trusts,... none of the natives, though they might be more powerful, attempted to rise in rebellion; or if such a thing ever did take place, the town where the revolt broke out was punished, and the ringleaders were sent prisoners to Cuzco....

All men so feared the king, that they did not dare to speak evil even of his shadow. And this was not all. If any of the king's captains or servants went forth to visit a distant part of the empire on some business, the people came out on the road with presents to receive them, not daring, even if one came alone, to omit to comply with all his commands.

So great was the veneration that the people felt for their princes, throughout this vast region, that every district was as well regulated and governed as if the lord was actually present to chastise those who acted contrary to his rules. This fear arose from the known valor of the lords and their strict justice. It was felt to be certain that those who did evil would receive punishment without fail, and that neither prayers nor bribes wold avert it. At the same time, the Incas always did good to those who were under their sway, and would not allow them to be ill-treated, nor that too much tribute should be exacted from them. Many who dwelt in a sterile country where they and their ancestors had lived with difficulty, found that through the orders of the Inca their lands were made fertile and abundant, the things being supplied which before were wanting. In other districts, where there was scarcity of clothing, owing to the people having no flocks, orders were given that cloth should be abundantly provided. In short, it will be understood that these lords knew how to enforce service and the payment of tribute, so they provided for the maintenance of the people, and took care that they should want for nothing. Through these good works, and because the lord always gave women and rich gifts to his principal vassals, he gained so much on their affections that he was most fondly loved....

One of the things which I admired most, in contemplating and noting down the affairs of this kingdom, was to think how and in what manner they can have made such grand and admirable roads as we now see, and what a number of men would suffice for their construction, and with what tools and instruments they can have leveled the mountains and broken through the rocks to make them so broad and good as they are. For it seems to me that if the King of Spain should desire to give orders for another royal road to be made, like that which goes from Quito to Cuzco, ...with all his power I believe that he could not get it done; nor could any force of men achieve such results unless there was also the perfect order by means of which the commands of the Incas were carried into execution....

TEXTUAL QUESTIONS FOR ANALYSIS

1. Describe in your own words the manner in which the Inca rulers were able to achieve a high degree of unity and obedience in their empire, according to the author.
2. What does the praise of the Inca highway system by de Leon imply about the roads of 16th century Spain and Europe?
3. Contrast the methods of Inca rule with those of the Aztecs as presented in your text. Which do you believe was the more effective, and why?
5. Although Pedro Cieza de Leon obviously found much to admire about the Inca civilization, he was a direct and active participant in its destruction. How do you think he justified to himself his apparently contradictory ideas and conduct?

Source: Harriet de Onis, trans. and Victor W. Von Hagen, ed., *The Incas of Pedro de Cieza de Leon* (Norman, Oklahoma: University of Oklahoma Press, 1959), pp. 165-167, 169-170.

CHAPTER 22
ORDINARY LIFE AMONG THE NON-WESTERN PEOPLES

Descriptions of ordinary life among non-Western peoples from the period of the first through the fifteenth century (the period covered by this chapter) are not plentiful, for the culture of the East was dominated, even to a greater degree than that of the West, by powerful imperial courts and their elaborate bureaucracies. But the largest cities in the world and the greatest concentrations of wealth were to be found in Asia during this period, so any information we do have on how life was actually lived in the great cities of India and China is of great value to the historian. The following selection has come down to us as an anonymous composition from the year 1235, describing the city of Hangzhou, capital city of the Southern Song Dynasty. From the amount of detail concerning markets and commerce, it is assumed that the author was probably a young merchant compiling an account for his employer. At any rate, present day historians are grateful for his eye for detail and his concentration upon the daily fe of the common people. Hangzhou was a port city located on the southern bank of the Yangtze River, and had become the Song capital in the mid-12th century when the Jurchen steppe nomads had invaded northern China. This region was the most densely populated area of China at that time, and with a population of over one million and an area of eight square miles, this Chinese imperial capital was probably the largest and richest urban center in the world.

A RECORD OF MUSINGS ON THE EASTERN CAPITAL

MARKETS- During the morning hours, markets extend from Tranquility Gate of the palace all the way to the north and south sides of the New Boulevard. Here we find pearl, jade, talismans, exotic plants and fruits, seasonal catches from the sea, wild game- all the rarities of the world seem to be gathered here. The food and commodity markets at Heavenly-View Gate, River Market Place, Central Square, Ba Creek, the end of Superior Lane, Tent Place, and Universal Peace Bridge are all crowded and full of traffic.

In the evening, with the exception of the square in front of the palace, the markets are as busy as during the day. The most attractive one is at Central Square, where all sorts of exquisite artifacts, instruments, containers, and hundreds of varieties of goods are for sale. In other marketplaces, sales, auctions, and exchanges go on constantly. In the wine shops and inns business thrives. Only after midnight does the city gradually quiet down, but before dawn, court officials already start preparing for audiences, and merchants are getting ready for the morning market once again. This cycle goes on all year round without respite....

On the lot in front of the wall of the city building, there are always various acting troupes performing, and this usually attracts a large crowd. The same kind of activity is seen in almost any vacant lot, including those at the meat market of the Great Common, the herb market at Charcoal Bridge, the book market at Orange Grove, the vegetable market on the east side of the city, and the rice market on the north side. There are many more interesting markets, such as the candy center at the Five Buildings, but I cannot name them all.

COMMERCIAL ESTABLISHMENTS- In general, the capital attracts the greatest variety of goods and has the best craftsmen... Some of the most famous specialties of the capital are the sweet-bean soup at the Miscellaneous Market, the pickled dates of the Ge family, the thick soup of the Guang family at Superior Lane, ... the cooked meats in front of Eternal Mercy Temple, Sister Song's fish broth at Penny Pond Gate, the juicy lungs at Flowing Gold Gate, ... the boots of the Peng family, the fine clothing of the Xuan family, the sticky rice pastry of the Zhang family, the flutes made by Gu the Fourth, and the Qiu family's Tatar whistles at the Great Commons.

WINE SHOPS- Among the various kinds of wine shops, the tea-and-food shops sell not only wine, but also various foods to go with it. However, to get seasonal delicacies not available in these shops, one should go to the inns, for they also have a menu from which one can make selections. The pastry-and-wine shops sell pastries with duckling and goose fillings, various fixings of pig tripe, intestines and blood, fish fat and spawn; but they are rather expensive.... The "luxuriant inns" have prostitutes residing in them, and the wine chambers are equipped with beds. At the gate of such an inn, on top of the red gardenia lantern, there is always a cover made of bamboo leaves. Rain or shine, this cover is always present, serving as a trademark. In other inns, the girls only keep the guests company. If a guest has other wishes, he has to go to the girl's place....

The expenses incurred on visiting an inn can vary widely. If you order food, but no drinks, it is called "having the lowly soup-and-stuff," and is quite inexpensive... However, if you ask for female company, then it is most likely that the girls will order the most expensive delicacies. You are well advised to appear shrewd and experienced, so as not to be robbed....

TEAHOUSES- In large teahouses, there are usually paintings and calligraphies by famous artists on display. In the old capital, only restaurants had them, to enable their patrons to while away the time as the food was being prepared, but now it is customary for teahouses as well to display paintings and the like....

Often young men gather in teahouses to practice singing or playing musical instruments. To give such amateur performances is called "getting posted."

A "social teahouse" is more of a community gathering place than a mere place that sells tea. Often tea-drinking is but an excuse, and people are rather generous when it comes to tips.

There is a special kind of teahouse where pimps and gigolos hang out. Another kind is occupied by people from various trades and crafts who use them as places to hire help, buy apprentices, and conduct business. These teahouses are called "trade heads."

"Water teahouses" are in fact pleasure houses, the tea being a cover. Some youths are quite willing to spend their money there, which is called "dry tea money."....

TEXTUAL QUESTIONS FOR ANALYSIS

1. Compare this description with that of the young Persian nobleman of Baghdad in Chapter Seventeen. What are similarities and differences in their descriptions of Baghdad and Hangzhou? Why is it obvious that the Chinese author is not a member of the aristocracy?
2. Identify and describe similarities between late twentieth century Western cities and thirteenth century Hangzhou?
3. According to his description, how were most businesses organized and conducted?
4. What do you think would be the main differences between a large European city of the thirteenth century such as London or Paris and Hangzhou?

Source: Patricia B. Ebrey, ed., *Chinese Civilization and Society: A Sourcebook* (New York: Free Press, 1981), pp. 100-102, 104-105.

CHAPTER 23
THE HIGH MEDIEVAL AGE

The crusades were an expression of the growing power and confidence of the societies of Western Europe, as nobility from throughout France, the German states, and England took up the cause of reconquering the Holy Land from the Muslims. Motivated by religious piety and a secular quest for land and wealth, these expeditions brought Roman Catholic Christianity into close contact for the first time with Islamic civilization and the Orthodox Christianity of the Byzantine Empire. Starting with the First Crusade in 1096-1099, there were eventually nine expeditions to the East, the final one ending in failure in 1271. By far the most successful was the First Crusade, which conquered Jerusalem and established a Christian kingdom in the Holy Land that lasted almost a century. The last Christian stronghold, the coastal city of Acre held out until 1291. The crusades were officially initiated by Pope Urban II in 1095 at the Council of Clermont. The Pope had received a request for assistance from the Byzantine Emperor Alexius Commenus against the Seljuk Turks, who had taken most of Anatolia from the Byzantine Empire. The Holy Land had been conquered by the Muslims in the seventh century, but the Islamic policy of religious toleration had allowed Christians to go on pilgrimage there for over three centuries. The Emperor claimed that these new Islamic warriors not only threatened the survival of the only Christian state in the East, but also would eliminate Christian entry into the Holy Land. The following selection is the account recorded by Robert the Monk of the speech made by Pope Urban II at the conclusion of the Council of Clermont. Less than four years after this call to holy war against the Muslims, a Christian army would conquer the city of Jerusalem, carry out a massacre of Muslims and Jews in the city, and establish the first Christian kingdom in ancient Palestine since the seventh century. As you read this selection, notice the justification given by Pope for the idea of a war of reconquest.

POPE URBAN II'S SPEECH AT CLERMONT, 1095

In the year of our Lord's Incarnation one thousand and ninety-five, a great council was celebrated within the bounds of Gaul (France), in Auvergne, in the city which is called Clermont. Over this Pope Urban II presided, with the Roman bishops and cardinals. This council was a famous one on account of the concourse of both French and German bishops, and of princes as well. Having arranged the matters relating to the Church, the lord pope went forth to a certain spacious plain, for no building was large enough to hold all the people. The pope then, with sweet and persuasive eloquence, addressed those present in words something like the following saying:

"Oh, race of Franks (people from France), race from across the mountains, race beloved and chosen by God- as is clear from many of your works- set apart from all other nations by the situation of your country as well as by your Catholic faith and the honor which you render to the holy Church: to you our discourse is addressed, and for you our exhortations are intended. We wish you to know what a grievous cause has led us to your country, for it is the imminent peril threatening you and all the faithful which has brought us hither.

"From the confines of Jerusalem and from the city of Constantinople a grievous report has gone forth and has repeatedly been brought to our ears; namely, that a race from the kingdom of the Persians, an accursed race, a race wholly alienated from God...., has violently invaded the lands of those Christians and has depopulated them by pillage and fire. They have led away a part of the captives into their own country, and a part they have killed by cruel tortures. They have either destroyed the churches of God or appropriated them for the rites of their own religion. They destroy the altars, after having defiled them with their uncleanness.... The kingdom of the Greeks (the Byzantine Empire) is now dismembered by them and has been deprived of territory so vast in extent that it could not be traversed in two months' time.

"On whom, therefore, is the labor of avenging these wrongs and of recovering this territory incumbent, if not upon you- you, upon whom, above all other nations, God has conferred remarkable glory in arms, great courage, bodily activity, and strength to humble the heads of those who resist you.... Let the holy sepulcher of our Lord and Savior, which is possessed by the unclean nations, especially arouse you, and the holy places which are now treated with ignominy and irreverently polluted with the filth of the unclean.

"....Let none of your possessions retain you, nor solicitude for your family affairs. For this land which you inhabit, shut in on all sides by the seas and surrounded by the mountain peaks, is too narrow for your large population; nor does it abound in wealth; and it furnishes scarcely food enough for its cultivators. Hence it is that you murder and devour one another, that you wage war, and that very many among you perish in internal strife.

"Let hatred therefore depart from among you, let your quarrels end, let wars cease, and let all dissentions and controversies slumber. Enter upon the road to the Holy Sepulcher; wrest that land from the wicked race, and subject it to yourselves. That land which.... was given by God into the power of the children of Israel. Jerusalem is the center of the earth; the land is fruitful above all others, like another paradise of delights. This spot the Redeemer of mankind has made illustrious by his advent, has beautified by his sojourn, has consecrated by his passion, has redeemed by his death, has glorified by his burial.

"This royal city, however, situated at the center of the earth, is now held captive by the enemies of Christ and is subjected, by those who do not know God, to the worship of the heathen. She seeks, therefore, and desires to be liberated and ceases not to implore you to come to her aid. From you especially she asks succor, because, as we have already said, God has conferred upon you above all nations great glory in arms. Accordingly, undertake this journey eagerly for the remission of your sins, with the assurance of the reward of imperishable glory in the kingdom of heaven."

TEXTUAL QUESTIONS FOR ANALYSIS

1. Why was Jerusalem so important, according to Pope Urban II?
2. What are the religious reasons he lists for embarking on this crusade, and what are the secular reasons?
3. What is the irony of his call for the French nobility to cease their internal warfare? What is the religious prize that he promises to all that take up this crusade?
4. Assume you are the Muslim ruler of Jerusalem. Compose a response to this speech.

Source: Oliver J. Thatcher and Edgar H. McNeal, eds., *A Source Book for Medieval History* (New York: Charles Scribner's Sons, 1905), pp. 518-521.

CHAPTER 24
LATE MEDIEVAL TROUBLES

The Babylonian Captivity and the Great Schism lowered the prestige and reduced the authority of the Roman Catholic Church and the Papacy in the fourteenth and early fifteenth century. For seventy years the Papacy in Avignon was notable for its incessant attempt to increase Papal revenues, not its moral authority. Then, from 1378 to 1417, the Church was divided, with competing Popes claiming authority in Rome and Avignon, and hurling edicts of excommunication at each other and their respective followers. The conciliar movement was an attempt by Church reformers to heal this schism by having broadly based Church councils debate the issues, and reach a solution through a process of prayer, deliberation, and voting. The central idea of these reformers was that ultimate authority in Church affairs should reside in such councils, and that a reduction in the power of the Papacy would be beneficial to the Church. In 1409 a group of reforming bishops succeeded in assembling a council in Pisa, Italy, to solve the problem of two Popes. The problem was worsened, however, when the council elected a new Pope, and the other two refused to step down. With three Popes now claiming to be the Vicar of Christ, the prestige and moral leadership of the Papacy continued to decline. After five years, a second great council was assembled in the German city of Constance to attempt a solution to the triple Papacy. This council represented the high point of the conciliar movement and did succeed in ending the Great Schism. The assembled clergy did not attempt to pick among the three incumbents, but elected a new Pope, Martin V. They also issued several decrees attempting to establish the idea of councils as superior to the authority of the Papacy, and to insure the frequent assembling of councils in the future. But within a few decades the new Pope and his successors in Rome had succeeded in repudiating the basic ideas of the Conciliar Movement, and reasserting Papal supremacy in Church affairs. The following selections are the two most important decrees issued by the Council of Constance and present a clear view of the ideas of the reformers.

THE DECREES OF THE COUNCIL OF CONSTANCE

DECREE SACROSANTCA

In the name of the Holy and indivisible Trinity; of the Father, Son, and Holy Ghost. Amen.

This holy synod of Constance, forming a general council for the extirpation of the present schism and the union and reformation, in head and members, of the church of God, legitimately assembled in the Holy Ghost, to the praise of Omnipotent God, in order that it may the more easily, safely, effectively and freely bring about the union and reformation of the church of God, hereby determines, decrees, ordains and declares what follows:-

It first declares that this same council, legitimately assembled in the Holy Ghost, forming a general council and representing the Catholic Church militant, has its power immediately from Christ, and everyone, whatever his state or position, even if it be the Papal dignity itself, is bound to obey it in all those things which pertain to the faith and the healing of the said schism, and to the general reformation of the Church of God, in head and members.

It further declares that anyone, whatever his condition, station or rank, even if it be the Papal, who shall contumaciously refuse to obey the mandates, decrees, ordinances or instructions which have been or shall be issued by this holy council, or by any other general council, legitimately summoned, which concern, or in any way relate to the above mentioned objects, shall, unless he repudiate his conduct, be subjected to condign penance and be suitably punished, having recourse, if necessary, to the other resources of the law.

DECREE FREQUENS

A frequent celebration of general councils is an especial means for cultivating the field of the Lord and effecting the destruction of briars, thorns, and thistles, to-wit, heresies, errors, and schism, and of bringing forth a most abundant harvest. The neglect to summon these, fosters and develops all these evils, as may be plainly seen from a recollection of the past and a consideration of existing conditions. Therefore, by a perpetual edict, we sanction, decree, establish and ordain that general councils shall be celebrated in the following manner, so that the next one shall follow the close of this present council at the end of five years. The second shall follow the close of that, at the end of seven years and councils shall thereafter be celebrated every ten years in such places as the Pope shall be required to designate and assign, with the consent and approbation of the council, one month before the close of the council in question, or which, in his absence, the council itself shall designate. Thus, with a certain continuity, a council will always be either in session, or be expected at the expiration of a definite time.

TEXTUAL QUESTIONS FOR ANALYSIS

1. Why do you think the reformers put their faith for the reform of the Church in the idea of periodic councils? Why do you think Popes resisted the idea?
2. What is the basis of the claim that the authority of a council is superior to that of a Pope?
3. Why do you think that they wanted the next council within five years, the next one within seven years, and after that at ten year intervals?
4. What do you think would have been the effect on the Church if their decrees had been honored?

Source: James Harvey Robinson, ed., *Translations and Reprints from the Original Sources of European History* (Philadelphia: University of Pennsylvania Press, 1902), Vol. 3, No. 6, pp. 31-32.

CHAPTER 25
THE EUROPEAN RENAISSANCE

Humanism must be considered the first and most persistent of the new movements that shaped the culture and society of the Renaissance. It began in Italy in the fourteenth century with a revival of interest in the lives and works of the ancients as models for morality, and soon led to the creation of new styles in painting, sculpture, and architecture as artists sought to understand, emulate, and improve upon the Greeks and Romans. As this new intellectual movement spread northward it sparked an interest in classical scholarship and criticism of the immorality and abuses that existed within society in general and the Church in particular. These northern humanists believed in rationalism as a guide to reforming the Church and society. They applauded what they perceived to be the rationality of the ancients and decried the gross superstitions and reliance on inherited tradition that they believed had been the mainstays of the Church and secular society for hundreds of years. One of the most influential of the northern humanists was the Dutch priest Desiderius Erasmus. He was a great critic of the abuses that he saw in the Catholic Church, and sought to reform it form within. He was a prolific writer, and the following selection is from one of his best known works, THE PRAISE OF FOLLY. This satire was published in 1509, and in it he criticized abuses and practices of the Church in hopes of promoting a more humane and rational spirituality.

THE PRAISE OF FOLLY

The next to be placed among the regiment of fools are such as make a trade of telling or inquiring after incredible stories of miracles and prodigies. Never doubting that a lie will choke them, they will muster up a thousand strange relations of spirits, ghosts, apparitions, raising of the devil , and such like bugbears of superstition; which the farther they are from being probably true, the more greedily they are swallowed, and the more devoutly believed. And these absurdities do not only bring an empty pleasure and cheap divertissement, but they are a good trade and procure a comfortable income to such priests and friars as by this craft get their gain.

To these again are nearly related such others as attribute strange virtues to all the shrines and images of saints and martyrs, and so would make their credulous proselytes believe that if they pay their devotion to St. Christopher in the morning, they shall be guarded and secured the day following from all dangers and misfortunes. If soldiers, when they first take arms, shall come and mumble over such a set prayer before the picture of St. Barbara, they shall return safe from all engagements.... The Christians have now their gigantic St. George, as well as the pagans had their Hercules; they paint the saint on horseback, and drawing the horse in splendid trapping very gloriously accounted, they scarce refrain in a literal sense from worshipping the very beast.

What shall I say of such as cry up and maintain the cheat of pardons and indulgences? That by these compute the time of each soul's residence in purgatory, and assign them a longer or shorter continuance, according as they purchase more or fewer of these paltry pardons and saleable exemptions? Or what can be said bad enough of others, who pretend that by the force of such magical charms, or by the fumbling over their beads in the rehearsal of such, and such petitions; which some religious imposters invented, either for diversion, or, what is more likely, for advantage; they shall procure riches, honor, pleasure, health, long life, lusty old age, nay, after death a sitting at the right hand of our Saviour in His kingdom.

By this easy way of purchasing pardons, any notorious highwayman, any plundering soldier, or any bribe-taking judge shall disburse some part of their unjust gains, and so think their grossest impieties sufficiently atoned for. So many perjuries, lusts, drunkenness, quarrels, bloodsheds, cheats, treacheries, shall all be, as it were, struck a bargain for, and such a contract made, as if they had paid off all arrears and might now begin upon a new score....

And now for some reflections upon popes, cardinals and bishops, who in pomp and splendor have almost equaled if not outdone secular princes. Now if anyone consider that their upper crotchet of white linen is to signify their unspotted purity and innocence; that their forked mitres, with both divisions tied together by the same knot, are to denote the joint knowledge of the Old and New Testament. That their always wearing gloves represents their keeping their hands clean and undefiled from lucre and covetousness; that the pastoral staff implies the care of a flock committed to their charge; that the cross carried before them expresses their victory over all carnal affection. He that considers this, and much more of the like nature, must needs conclude they are entrusted with a very weighty and difficult office. But alas, they think it sufficient if they can but feed themselves, and as to their flock, either commend them to the care of Christ Himself, or commit them to the guidance of some inferior vicars and curates. They do not so much as remember what their name of bishop imports, to wit, labor, pains and diligence, but by base simoniacal contracts, they are in a profane sense... overseers of their own gain and income.

The popes of Rome... pretend themselves Christ's vicars; if they would but imitate His exemplary life.... an unintermittent course of preaching and attendance with poverty, nakedness, hunger and a contempt of this world; if they did but consider the import of the word pope, which signifies a father; or if they did but practice their surname of most holy, what order or degrees of men would be in a worse condition? There would be then no such vigorous making of parties and buying of votes in the conclave upon the vacancy of that see...

TEXTUAL QUESTIONS FOR ANALYSIS

1. What is his opinion of the practices of the Church of his day regarding prayers to saints and indulgences? How is he at variance with the established practice of the Church?
2. What is wrong with the bishops of his day? What should they be doing?
3. What does he see wrong with the Pope?
4. What were the obstacles to the changes he wanted to see? Although unintentional, how might his criticisms have hastened the Reformation?

Source: Desiderus Erasmus, *In Praise of Folly* (London: Reeves and Turner, 1876), pp. 81-82, 134-135.

CHAPTER 26
A LARGER WORLD OPENS

Portugal was the country that led the way in the exploration and exploitation of West Africa from the mid-fifteenth century. Initially attempting to gain access to India, the Portugese soon discovered that Africa was vastly larger than they had anticipated, and that the gold and slave trade of West Africa, monopolized for centuries by Arab caravans crossing the Sahara, could be enormously profitable. The result was the creation of a string of trading bases along the coast, and by 1500 about 10,000 slaves and a half-ton of gold annually were arriving in Lisbon. From there the slaves were either sold to the Arab states of North Africa or shipped across the Atlantic to the new sugar plantations of the Caribbean and South America. The essential requirement for the Portugese and all other European states that established trading bases on the African coasts were African rulers that were willing to be partners in this trade. The political and military strength of the West African states, the variety of diseases to which Europeans had no immunity, and the absence of safe and fast inland transportation meant that the Portugese and other European states involved in West African trade were not able to penetrate into the interior of Africa until the nineteenth century. The Europeans came as traders, not colonizers or conquerors, and they depended on establishing mutually beneficial trading arrangements with local African rulers for goods and slaves.

The largest West African state at the beginning of the sixteenth century was the kingdom of Kongo, located along the banks of the Congo River and along the coast of what is today Angola and Zaire. The Portuguese established a trading base there in 1483, and immediately began to court the royal family. King Nzinga a Kuwu of Kongo sent court officials and members of the royal family to Lisbon to learn about European civilization, and the Portuguese sent missionaries, artisans, and soldiers to Kongo to assist the king in his wars with his neighbors. The captives from these wars became the basis of the slave trade in Kongo. In 1506, Nzinga Mbemba, the Christian son of King Kuwu, succeeded his father and ruled till 1543. He took the Christian name of King Afonso I and promoted the spread of European culture into his kingdom by adopting Christianity as the state religion, copying Portuguese court etiquette, and using Portuguese as the official language of the royal court. He imported European weapons, technology, and domestic animals, paying for these by the gold and slave trade, and aspired to make Kongo the most powerful and prosperous kingdom of West Africa. By the time he died, however, royal authority had declined and other local rulers were establishing themselves as competitors, largely through the wealth and weapons they had gained by selling slaves and gold directly to the Portuguese. The introduction of European products and customs, and the constant efforts by the Portuguese to increase the slave trade had destabilized the kingdom, and undermined the authority of the king. King Afonso recognized the threat produced by the Portuguese, and in 1526 wrote the following letters to King Joao III of Portugal in an attempt to remedy the situation. Written in Portuguese by African secretaries, they are the earliest existing African commentaries on the European impact. They are part of a total of twenty-four letters that he wrote to two Portuguese kings on a variety of subjects

LETTERS OF AFONSO I TO THE KING OF PORTUGAL

Sir, Your Highness should know how our Kingdom is being lost in so many ways that it is convenient to provide for the necessary remedy, since this is caused by the excessive freedom given by your agents and officials to the men and merchants who are allowed to come to this Kingdom to set up shops with goods and many things which have been prohibited by us, and which they spread throughout our Kingdoms and Domains in such an abundance that many of our vassals, who we had in obedience, do not comply because they have the things in greater abundance than we ourselves; and it was with these things that we had them content and subjected under our vassalage and jurisdiction, so it is doing a great harm not only to the service of God, but the security and peace of our Kingdoms and State as well.

And we cannot reckon on how great the damage is, since the mentioned merchants are taking every day our natives, sons of the land and the sons of our noblemen and vassals and our relatives, because the thieves and men of bad conscience grab them wishing to have the things and wares of this Kingdom which they are ambitious of; they grab them and get them to be sold; and so great, Sir, is the corruption and licentiousness that our country is being completely depopulated, and Your Highness should not agree with this nor accept it as in your service....

Moreover, Sir, in our Kingdoms there is another great inconvenience which is of little service to God, and this is that many of our people, keenly desirous as they are of the wares and things of your Kingdoms, which are brought here by your people, and in order to satisfy their voracious appetite, seize many of our people, freed and exempt men; and very often it happens that they kidnap even noblemen and the sons of noblemen, and our relatives, and take them to be sold to the white men who are in our Kingdoms; and for this purpose they have concealed them; and others are brought during the night so that they might not be recognized.

And as soon as they are taken by the white men they are immediately ironed and branded with fire, and when they are carried to be embarked, if they are caught by our guards' men the whites allege that they have bought them but they cannot say from whom, so that it is our duty to do justice and to restore to the freemen their freedom, but it cannot be done if your subjects feel offended, as they claim to be.

And to avoid such a great evil we passed a law so that any white man living in our Kingdoms and wanting to purchase goods in any way should first inform three of our noblemen and officials of our court whom we rely upon in this matter, and these are Dom Pedro Manipanza and Dom Manuel Manissaba, our chief usher, and Goncalo Pires our chief freighter, who should investigate if the mentioned goods (slaves) are captives or free men, and if cleared by them there will be no further doubt nor embargo for them to be taken and embarked. But if the white men do not comply with it they will lose the aforementioned goods. And if we do them this favor and concession it is for the part Your Highness has in it, since we know that it is in your service too that these goods are taken from our Kingdom, otherwise we should not consent to this.

Sir, Your Highness has been kind enough to write to us saying that we should ask in letters for anything we need, and that we shall be provided with everything, and as the peace and the health of our Kingdom depend on us, and as there are among us old folks and people who have lived for many days, it happens that we have continuously many and different diseases which put us very often in such weakness that we reach almost the last extreme; and the same happens to our children, relatives and natives owing to the lack in this country of physicians and surgeons who might know how to cure properly such diseases. And as we have got neither dispensaries nor drugs which might help us in this forlornness, many of those who had been already confirmed and instructed in the holy faith of Our Lord Jesus Christ perish and die; and the rest of the people in their majority cure themselves with herbs and breads and other ancient methods, so that they put all their faith in the mentioned herbs and ceremonies if they live, and believe that they are saved if they die; and this is not much in the service of God.

And to avoid such a great error and inconvenience, since it from God in the first place and then from your Kingdoms and from Your Highness that all the good and drugs and medicines have come to save us, we beg of you to be agreeable and kind enough to send us two physicians and two apothecaries and one surgeon, so that they may come with their drugstores and all the necessary things to stay in our kingdoms, because we are in extreme need of them all and each of them....We beg of Your Highness as a great favor to do this for us, because besides being good in itself it is in the service of God as we have said above.

TEXTUAL QUESTIONS FOR ANALYSIS

1. Describe in your own words the objections of King Afonso to the manner in which the slave trade was being conducted. How does he distinguish between legitimate and illegitimate trade in slaves?
2. Does King Afonso see the Portuguese trade and presence in his kingdom as a right or a privilege? What does he apparently consider to be the most important benefits of his kingdom's association with the Portuguese?
3. Given the medical standards of sixteenth century Europe, what does his plea for medical assistance from the Portuguese indicate about the medical standards of Kongo?
4. What are the elements of Portuguese culture that he obviously welcomes? How would you describe the general tone of these letters? Why?

Source: Basil Davidson, trans., *The African Past* (London: Curtis Brown, Ltd., 1964), pp. 20-25.

CHAPTER 27
THE PROTESTANT REFORMATION

Martin Luther is rightly regarded as the original founding father of the Protestant Reformation, but like most religious reformers, he did not start out to create a new religion or to destroy the old religion, although he ended up doing the former and attempting the latter. His first direct challenge to Church authority and practice came in October, 1517, when he posted his famous Ninety-five Theses on the door of the castle church in Wittenburg. But Luther was a professor of theology at the University of Wittenburg, and the posting of theses in a public place was the standard practice for those who wished to host a scholarly debate on any controversial subject. What he was doing was inviting Church officials to engage him in an open debate on indulgences, which he believed, both as a theologian and a practicing Catholic, could not be justified by scripture or by the manner in which the sale of indulgences was conducted by the Papacy. It is important to remember that what he was seeking in the posting of his theses was reform, not revolution. It was only later, when Church authorities condemned his ideas as heretical, that he was forced to go beyond debate.

LUTHER'S NINETY-FIVE THESES

Out of love and zeal for truth and the desire to bring it to light, the following theses will be publicly discussed at Wittenberg under the chairmanship of the reverend father Martin Luther, Master of Arts and Sacred Theology and regularly appointed Lecturer on these subjects at that place. He requests that those who cannot be present to debate orally with us will do so by letter.

In the Name of Our Lord Jesus Christ. Amen.
1. When Our Lord and Master Jesus Christ said, "Repent," he willed the entire life of believers to be one of repentance.
2. This word cannot be understood as referring to the sacrament of penance, that is, confession and satisfaction, as administered by the clergy.
3. Yet it does not mean solely inner repentance; such inner repentance is worthless unless it produces various outward mortifications of the flesh.
4. The penalty of sin remains as long as the hatred of self, that is, true inner repentance, until our entrance into the kingdom of heaven.
5. The pope neither desires nor is able to remit any penalties except those imposed by his own authority or that of the canons.
6. The pope cannot remit any guilt, except by declaring and showing that it has been remitted by God; or, to be sure, by remitting guilt in cases reserved to his judgment. If his right to grant remission in these cases were disregarded, the guilt would certainly remain unforgiven.
13. The dying are freed by death from all penalties, are already dead as far as the canon laws are concerned, and have a right to be released from them.
23. If remission of all penalties whatsoever could be granted to anyone at all, certainly it would be granted only to the most perfect, that is, to very few.
24. For this reason most people are necessarily deceived by that indiscriminate and high-sounding promise of release from penalty.
25. That power which the pope has in general over purgatory corresponds to the power which any bishop or curate has in a particular way in his own diocese or parish.
26. The pope does very well when he grants remission to souls in purgatory, not by the power of the keys, which he does not have, but by way of intercession for them.
27. They preach only human doctrines who say that as soon as he money clinks into the money chest, the soul flies out of purgatory.
28. It is certain that when money clinks in the money chest, greed and avarice can be increased; but when the church intercedes, the result is in the hands of God alone.
32. Those who believe that they can be certain of their salvation because they have indulgence letters will be eternally damned, together with their teachers.
33. Men must especially be on their guard against those who say that the pope's pardons are that inestimable gift of God by which man is reconciled to him.
35. They who teach that contrition is not necessary on the part of those who intend to buy souls out of purgatory or to buy confessional privileges preach unchristian doctrine.
37. Any true Christian, whether living or dead, participates in all the blessings of Christ and the church; and this is granted him by God, even without indulgence letters.

38. Nevertheless, papal remission and blessing are by no means to be disregarded, for they are, as I have said, the proclamation of the divine remission.
41. Papal indulgences must be preached with caution, lest people erroneously think that they are preferable to other good works of love.
42. Christians are to be taught that the pope does not intend that the buying of indulgences should in any way be compared with works of mercy.
46. Christians are to be taught that, unless they have more than they need, they must reserve enough for their family needs and by no means squander it on indulgences.
47. Christians are to be taught that the buying of indulgences is a matter of free choice, not commanded.
50. Christians are to be taught that if the pope knew the exactions of the indulgence preachers, he would rather that the basilica of St. Peter were burned to ashes than built up with the skin, flesh, and bones of his sheep.
51. Christians are to be taught that the pope would and should wish to give of his own money, even though he had to sell the basilica of St. Peter, to many of those from whom certain hawkers of indulgences cajole money.
52. It is vain to trust in salvation by indulgence letters, even though the indulgence commissary, or even the pope, were to offer his soul as security.
79. To say that the cross emblazoned with the papal coat of arms, and set up by the indulgence preachers, is equal in worth to the cross of Christ is blasphemy.
80. The bishops, curates, and theologians who permit such talk to be spread among the people will have to answer for this.
81. The unbridled preaching of indulgences makes it difficult even for learned men to rescue the reverence which is due the pope from slander or from the shrewd questions of the laity.
90. To repress these very sharp questions of the laity by force alone, and not to resolve them by giving reasons, is to expose the church and the pope to the ridicule of their enemies and to make Christians unhappy.

TEXTUAL QUESTIONS FOR ANALYSIS

1. According to Luther, what is wrong with the practice of selling indulgences and the manner in which the selling is conducted? How would he like to see the practice operate?
2. From the tone and content of these theses, does he identify himself as a friend or enemy of the Church and the Pope? Explain and give examples.
3. In what ways does he dispute the authority of the Pope and in what areas does he accept the Pope's authority?
4. Although intended as a basis for debate, if Luther's theses had been accepted, what do you think would have been the effect? What later Protestant doctrines are apparent in these theses?

Source: Harold J. Grimm, ed., *Luther's Works* (Philadelphia: Muhlenberg Press, 1957), Vol. 31, pp. 25-30, 32-33.

CHAPTER 28
FOUNDATIONS OF THE EUROPEAN STATES

Royal absolutism became the prevailing political system and doctrine of most European states in the sixteenth and seventeenth centuries. This concentration of power and authority in royal hands was supported by both secular political theorists and religious authorities. One of the major results of the Reformation was the creation of state churches. The political power of the Catholic Church was removed in northern Europe by the rise of Protestantism, and in those areas remaining Catholic, the threat of conversion and the need for a monarch's protection achieved the same result. Thus, unlike the middle ages when the Church had been a rival and contender for power against monarchs, by the 1600's religious leaders looked upon monarchs as protectors and defenders of their rights and privileges. This system of mutual support and admiration worked well for monarchs, as support for their position was sanctified by church authorities, and opposition to them was equated with heresy.

Louis XIV was and is rightly regarded as the very epitome of royal absolutism, and one of his strongest defenders was Jacques Bossuet, Bishop of Meaux (1627-1704). Bishop Bossuet was an enormously popular preacher and writer whose royalist essays and sermons brought him to the king's attention. Louis was so impressed that he made the bishop the tutor to his eldest son, and awarded him a royal pension. Bossuet responded by writing essays like the following which constitute an extreme defense of absolutism on the basis of Divine Right. The bishop's thesis was consciously unmaterialistic and admittedly unscientific, for he used only scripture to justify his belief that royal authority represented God's authority on earth. A king's rule was sacred because it was derived from God; and the state and the monarch were one, as shown in Holy Scripture. Only the king had God's authority to rule, and the people were assigned the duty of blind obedience. The following selection is from an essay published by Bishop Bossuet in 1679, and dedicated to the Dauphin, the king's son and successor.

POLITICS DRAWN FROM THE VERY WORDS OF HOLY SCRIPTURE

There are four characteristics or qualities essential to royal authority:
First of all royal authority is sacred;
Secondly it is paternal;
Thirdly it is absolute;
Fourthly it is subject to reason.

God establishes kings to be his ministers and to rule over his peoples, and all power comes from God. "The prince," said Saint Paul, "is God's minister for the good of all. If you do evil, tremble; for it is not in vain that he has the sword: and he is the minister of God, the avenger of wrong doing." Princes therefore act as ministers of God, and as his lieutenants on earth. It is through them that He administers his empire.... It is for this reason that the royal throne is not the throne of man, but the throne of God himself....

It appears from this that the person of the king is sacred, and that to make an attempt against him is an act of sacrilege.

Through his prophets God has anointed kings with a sacred unction, as he has anointed his pontiffs and his altars. But even without the outward application of this unction, kings are sacred by their office, being the representatives of the divine majesty. They are deputies by act of providence for the execution of His designs.... The title Christ is given to kings, and one sees them everywhere called Christs or the anointed of God....

Even though kings may not acquit themselves of their duty, one must respect them in their office and their ministry. "Obey your masters, not only the ones who are good and moderate, but even those who are troublesome and unjust." There is even something religious about the respect that one renders to a prince. The service of God and the respect for kings are one and the same thing; Saint Peter put these two duties together: "Fear God, honor the king." God has also put something divine in princes. "I have said: You are gods, and you are all children of God."....

Kings must respect their own power, and employ it only for the public good. Their power, coming from on high,.... must be used with fear and caution as a thing that emanates from God and for which God will hold them accountable.... Kings must therefore tremble in using the power that God gives to them, and ponder over how horrible is the sacrilege of misusing a power that comes from God.

We have seen kings seated upon the throne of the Lord, provided with the sword that he has placed into their hands. What profanity and audacity it is for kings to sit upon the throne that God has given to them and hinder His laws by using the sword that He has placed into their hands to do violence and to cut the throats of His children. Let them therefore respect their power, because it not their power, but the power of God, which they must use in a saintly and religious fashion....

We have already seen that kings take the place of God who is the true father of the human species. We have also seen that the first idea of power which existed among men was paternal authority; kings were made on the model of fathers. Everyone is also in agreement that the obedience which is due to public authority is found in the Ten Commandments- in the precept which obliges one to honor his parents. It seems from all of this that the title of King is the title of father and that goodness is the most natural characteristic of kings....

God, who has made all men's bodies from the same earth, and has equally put in their souls the image of his resemblance, has not established among them so many distinctions in order to have on one side the proud and on the other slaves and miserable people. He has made the great to protect the little; He has given His power to kings in order for them to procure the public good and to support the people....

TEXTUAL QUESTIONS FOR ANALYSIS

1. According to Bossuet what are the chief duties of a king and his subjects? In family terms, what is a king supposed to emulate?
2. Bossuet contends that a king should be just and fair in his rule, but what should his subjects do if a king is a tyrant?
3. What is the source of a king's authority and to whom must a king answer for his actions?
4. According to Bossuet, is government divine or secular in origin? What are a king's qualifications?

Source: Brian Tierney, Donald Kegan, and L. Pearce Williams, eds., *Great Issues in Western Civilization*, 3rd ed. (New York: Random House, 1976), Vol. 2, pp. 613-615.

CHAPTER 29
EAST EUROPEAN EMPIRES

Peter the Great has long been considered a pivotal figure in Russian history. He inherited a monarchy and kingdom that had been relatively isolated from Western Europe for several centuries, and that was regarded by most westerners as backward, poor, and barely civilized. The few Westerners who visited Russia before Peter were decidedly unimpressed, and often wrote travel accounts that emphasized the boorishness of the Russian nobility, and the public drunkenness that was a feature of court functions. Peter the Great, for good or ill, changed the perception and the reality of Russia. He re-oriented Russia from a predominately Asiatic state into a European power. His new capital city reflected this Western orientation in its architecture, and his government copied Western models of structure and administration. By defeating Sweden, he gained territory in the West that gave Russia a new status and interest in European affairs. Building on the traditional political and religious authority of the Tsar, he became a more powerful absolute monarch than even Louis XIV, to the extent of even forcing the Russian nobility to shave their beards and give up their traditional long robes for Western trousers and waist coats. At the center of these changes was the Tsar himself; physically imposing at nearly seven feet in height, endowed with an insatiable curiosity about technical matters, he drove himself and his court with an urgency and energy that amazed foreign contemporaries. He could be both magnanimous and sadistically cruel, not only to defeated enemies but also to his own court and his own family. He remains to this day a paradoxical figure, but one whose importance to Russian history is undeniable. We know more about him than any earlier Tsar because he was the first Russian ruler to travel abroad and the first to encourage foreign business and diplomatic contact. Thus, we have a large number of contemporary accounts by Westerners who either met him on his travels abroad, or lived in Russia and wrote accounts of his activities. Both of the following accounts were written in 1698, during Peter's first trip abroad (1697-1698). The first is by Anglican Bishop Gilbert Burnett who met and talked with the Tsar on his visit to England. Burnett later published his memoirs, from which this account is taken. The second selection is from the diary of an Austrian diplomat, the Baron Von Korb, who was stationed in Moscow for several years. While Peter was abroad on his trip, his sister Sophia was involved in a rebellion against him led by the Streltsi, the Imperial guard.

BISHOP GILBERT BURNETT'S HISTORY

He is a man of very hot temper, soon inflamed and very brutal in his passion. He raises his natural heat by drinking much brandy, which he distills himself with great application. He is subject to convulsive motions all over his body, and his head seems to be affected with these. He wants not capacity, and has a larger measure of knowledge that might be expected from his education, which was very indifferent. A want of judgment, with an instability of temper, appear in him too often and too evidently.

He is mechanically turned, and seems designed by nature rather to be a ship carpenter than a great prince. This was his chief study and exercise while he stayed here. He wrought much with his own hands and made all about him work at the models of ships. He told me he designed a great fleet at Azov and with it he intended to attack the Turkish empire. But he did not seem capable of conducting so great a design, though his conduct in his wars since this has discovered a greater genius in him than appeared at this time.

...He was, indeed, resolved to encourage learning and to polish his people by sending some of them to travel in other countries and to draw strangers to come and live among them. He seemed apprehensive ever of his sister's (Princess Sophia) intrigues. There was a mixture both of passion and severity in his temper. He is resolute, but understands little of war, and seemed not at all inquisitive that way.

After I had seen him often, and had conversed much with him, I could not but adore the depth of the providence of God that had raised up such a furious man to so absolute an authority over so great a part of the world....

VON KORB'S DIARY

How sharp was the pain, how great the indignation, to which the Tsar's Majesty was mightily moved, when he knew of the rebellion of the Streltsi, betraying openly a mind panting for vengeance! He was still tarrying at Vienna, quite full of the desire of setting out for Italy; but fervid as was his curiosity of rambling abroad, it was, nevertheless, speedily extinguished on the announcement of the troubles that had broken out in the bowels of his realm.... Nor did he long delay the plan for his justly excited wrath; he took the quick post, as his ambassador suggested, and in four weeks' time he had got over about 1500 miles without accident, and arrived the 4th of September, 1698,- a monarch for the well disposed, but an avenger for the wicked.

His first anxiety after his arrival was about the rebellion,- in what it consisted, what the insurgents meant, who dared to instigate such a crime. And as nobody could answer accurately upon all points, and some pleaded their own ignorance, others the obstinacy of the Streltsi, he began to have suspicions of everybody's loyalty.... No day, holy or profane, were the inquisitors idle; every day was deemed fit and lawful for torturing. There were as many scourges as there were accused, every inquisitor was a butcher.... The whole month of October was spent in lacerating the backs of culprits with the knot and with flames; no day were those left alive exempt from scourging or scorching; or else they were broken upon the wheel, or driven to the gibbet, or slain with the ax....

In front of the nunnery where Sophia was confined there were thirty gibbets erected in a quadrangle shape, from which there hung two hundred and thirty Streltsi; the three principal ringleaders, who tendered a petition to Sophia touching the administration of the realm, were hanged close to the windows of the princess, presenting, as it were, the petitions that were placed in their hands, so near that Sophia might with ease touch them.

TEXTUAL QUESTIONS FOR ANALYSIS

1. What are the character traits of Peter that are portrayed in both accounts?
2. What are the best characteristics of Peter presented here and what are the worst? Which of these character traits made the greatest difference in Russian history?
3. Upon what basis, religious or secular, do you think Peter would have justified his rule? Why?
4. What is the tone of each description? Explain.

Source: J. H. Robinson, *Readings in European History* (Boston: Ginn and Co., 1906), Vol. 2, pp. 303-306, 310-312.

CHAPTER 30
CHINA FROM THE MING TO THE EARLY QING DYNASTY

The Ming dynasty (1368-1644) began as a period of growth and renewal for China under its founder, the peasant Emperor Hongwu. But by the early 1600's the Ming dynasty was in decline as emperors and their officials either ignored or failed to deal with new problems such as Manzhou pressure from the north, increasing pirate raids on the coast, and mounting banditry and rebellion in the outlying provinces. One of the reasons for this was the practice of Ming emperors giving increasing power to the court eunuchs. The founding Emperor Hongwu began the practice of using eunuchs as court advisers, believing them to be less corruptible than the Confucian scholars who had advised earlier dynasties due to their lack of family responsibilities. The practice had worked as long as the emperors had maintained tight control over their courts, but by the beginning of the seventeenth century the imperial government was divided into two major factions, those supporting the court eunuchs and those favoring the Confucian scholar-officials. Such factionalism, coupled with weak and incompetent emperors, proved fatal to the Ming dynasty.

The following selection is part of the official history of the Ming dynasty, written by the Qing historian Zhang Tingyu in 1739, over a century after the events it describes. It traces the rise and fall of the court eunuch Wei Zhingxian, providing us considerable insight into the problems that plagued the late Ming government. Zhang's account is clearly anti-eunuch, possibly due to the fact that he was a Confucian scholar, but it is regarded as factually accurate, and is considered today a major source for the history of the Ming dynasty.

HISTORY OF THE MING

Selected as a palace eunuch in the Wanli period (1573-1620), Wei Zhongxian moved quickly to ingratiate himself with those who could help his cause. An excellent cook, he was particularly patronized by Princess Wang, mother of the crown prince designate, later known as Emperor Ming Xizong. Subsequently he became a lover to the prince's wet nurse named Ke, who had abandoned an earlier lover on his behalf. As later events proved, this alliance between a eunuch and a wet nurse, based upon a relationship of illicit love, formed the basis of Wei Zhongxian's emergence to power.

Within a month after Ming Xizong's accession to the throne (1620), wet nurse Ke was titled Madame Fengsheng and eunuch Wei received three simultaneous appointments, including the appointment as administrator of rites. Normally only a man of great learning could be privileged to occupy that post; eunuch Wei acquired that post only because of Ke's insistence. Meanwhile the close relatives of both, including an elder brother of the eunuch, were promoted to lucrative positions and titled accordingly....

As long as Ke's influence over the emperor continued, Wei Zhongxian could do whatever he pleased with his rivals and enemies inside the palace. All of them, one after another, were ousted from positions of power and influence, including Ke's former lover previously mentioned. Having thus secured his own position inside the palace, Wei Zhongxian received permission from the emperor to train the eunuchs under his control in the use of military weapons and other martial arts. To keep the emperor busy, he led the young man to a variety of dissipations, such as sex, music, hunting, and gambling....

A political machine was thus established, which functioned effectively, though ruthlessly, throughout the empire.... The political machine was so pervasive that none of the cabinet ministers and governors-general, or any other high-ranking official, could hold his post for a single day without being a staunch member of the Grand Eunuch's clique....

Great though it was, the power of the Grand Eunuch fell as precipitously as it had risen. In the eighth month of the seventh year of Tian Ji (1627) Emperor Ming Xizong died and was succeeded by Prince Hsing who, after accession, was known as Emperor Ming Chongzhen (1627-1644). When serving as a crown prince, Chongzhen detested Grand Eunuch Wei for his evil ways but was careful enough not to offend him until he, upon becoming an emperor, could do something about his misgivings.... In the eleventh month of the same year the Grand Eunuch was exiled....

Shortly after the Grand Eunuch's exile, the emperor ordered a special prosecutor to proceed to Fengyang to question him about the crimes he had allegedly committed. Hearing about the impending arrival of the prosecutor, Grand Eunuch Wei,... hanged himself. The emperor ordered his head to be severed from his body and his body sliced as a posthumous punishment. Ke, the Grand Eunuch's longtime ally and friend, had already been executed.

TEXTUAL QUESTIONS FOR ANALYSIS

1. What were the steps by which the eunuch Wei rose to power within the Ming government?
2. What is the difference in theory and practice between a government of Confucian

scholar-officials and the system of personal rule of the Grand Eunuch Wei?
3. Based on your text and the above document, what was the larger significance of the power struggle between the court factions of the late Ming dynasty?
4. Summarize the lessons that the historian Zhang Tingyu probably hoped that the Qing emperors would gain from studying the late Grand Eunuch Wei?

Source: Dun J. Li, *The Civilization of China* (New York: Charles Scribner's Sons, 1975), pp. 242-248.

CHAPTER 31
JAPAN AND COLONIAL SOUTHEAST ASIA TO THE NINETEENTH CENTURY

The Tokugawa Shogunate brought peace and order to Japan after a century of civil war. It also made the samurai warrior class obsolete. In the seventeenth and eighteenth centuries, the samurai attempted to maintain their warrior traditions through elaborate display and government service. Much as European nobility attempted to develop a cult of chivalry after their real military function was taken over by professional armies, the Japanese samurai attempted to emphasize their unique position in society as a defense against their loss of prestige and position. Even though there were no more wars to fight, the cult of the samurai, with its insistence on the uncomplaining acceptance of hardship and total obedience and loyalty to one's lord, would continue to exert a powerful influence on Japanese society and culture.

This desire to preserve the essence of the samurai experience led to the publication of works that purported to describe exactly what it meant to be a samurai. There were few books on how to be a samurai before the seventeenth century. Apparently, on the job training was considered sufficient in the days when the samurai were the warrior class of feudal Japan. The following selection is one of the best examples of the pro-samurai literature of Tokugawa Japan, THE BOOK OF THE SAMURAI, written in 1716 by Yamamoto Tsunetomo (1659-1720). He came from a samurai family, and served for twenty-one years as scribe to the high-ranking samurai, Nabeshima Mitsushige, a provincial governor. Neither scribe nor lord ever fought in battle, but they did share a keen interest in literature. Following his lord's death, he became a Buddhist monk, and late in life dictated THE BOOK OF THE SAMURAI. He may not have been an actual warrior, but this warrior code had been central to his life, and he obviously wanted to preserve these ideals.

THE BOOK OF THE SAMURAI

Although it stands to reason that a samurai should be mindful of the Way of the Samurai, it would seem that we are all negligent. Consequently, if someone were to ask, "What is the true meaning of the Way of the Samurai?" the person who would be able to answer promptly is rare. This is because it has not been established in one's mind beforehand. From this, one's unmindfulness of the Way can be known....

The Way of the Samurai is found in death. When it comes to either/or, there is only the quick choice of death. It is not particularly difficult. Be determined and advance. To say that dying without reaching one's aim is to die a dog's death is the frivolous way of sophisticates. When pressed with the choice of life or death, it is not necessary to gain one's aim.

We all want to live. And in large part we make our logic according to what we like. But not having attained our aim and continuing to live is cowardice. This is a thin dangerous line. To die without gaining one's aim is a dog's death and fanaticism. But there is no shame in this. This is the substance of the Way of the Samurai. If by setting one's heart right every morning
and evening, one is able to live as though his body were already dead, he gains freedom in the Way. His whole life will be without blame, and he will succeed in his calling.

A man is a good retainer to the extent that he earnestly places importance in his master. This is the highest sort of retainer. If one is born into a prominent family that goes back for generations, it is sufficient to deeply consider the matter of obligation to one's ancestors, to lay down one's body and mind, and to earnestly esteem one's master. It is further good fortune if, more than this, one has wisdom and talent and can use them appropriately. But even a person who is good for nothing and exceedingly clumsy will be a reliable retainer if only he has the determination to think earnestly of his master. Having only wisdom and talent is the lowest tier of usefulness.

Being a retainer is nothing other than being a supporter of one's lord, entrusting matters of good and evil to him, and renouncing self-interest. If there are but two or three men of this type, the fief will be secure.

Every morning one should first do reverence to his master and parents and then to his patron deities and guardian Buddhas. If he will only make his master first in importance, his parents will rejoice and the gods and Buddhas will give their assent. For a warrior there is nothing other than thinking of his master. If one creates this resolution within himself, he will always be mindful of the master's person and will not depart from him even for a moment.

Moreover, a woman should consider her husband first, just as he considers his master first.

There are two things that will blemish a retainer, and these are riches and honor. If one but remains in modest circumstances, he will not be marred.

There was a man who said, "Such and such a person has a violent disposition, but this is what I said right to his face...." This was an unbecoming thing to say, and it was said simply because he wanted to be known as a rough fellow. It was rather low, and it can be seen that he was still rather immature. It is because a samurai has correct manners that he is admired. Speaking of other people in this way is no different from an exchange between low class spearmen. It is vulgar.

TEXTUAL QUESTIONS FOR ANALYSIS

1. What does Yamamoto consider to be the ideal qualities of a samurai?
2. What elements of Confucianism do you see in this description? Of Buddhism?

3. Even though the samurai were no longer essential, what role can they play society?

4. Would these samurai virtues continue to be important in Japan in the twentieth century? Give examples.

Source: Yamamoto Tsunetomo, *Hagakure (The Book of the Samurai)* (Tokyo: Kodansha International, Ltd., 1979), pp. 32-34.

CHAPTER 32
THE RISE AND FALL OF THE MUSLIM EMPIRES

Suleiman the Magnificent (1494-1566) was certainly one of the great world rulers of the sixteenth century. During the course of his forty-six year reign the Ottomans would reach the height of their influence and power. Unlike his predecessors who had concentrated on the Asiatic portions of the Ottoman Empire, Suleiman looked to Europe for additional areas of conquest. He mounted huge campaigns that conquered most of the Balkans, defeated and killed the King of Hungary, annexed large portions of that kingdom, and in 1529 laid siege to Vienna, the high-water mark of his European conquests. Small wonder that he was regarded with fear and awe by the Europeans of the sixteenth century.

One of the best contemporary European accounts of Suleiman is that of Ogier Ghiselin de Busbecq, a Flemish professional diplomat who served King Ferdinand of Hungary, the brother of Emperor Charles V of the Holy Roman Empire. Born in 1522, he entered diplomatic service about 1550, and served Ferdinand in London and Vienna. In 1554 he was sent to Constantinople to arrange a peace treaty between Ferdinand and Suleiman. He remained there for eight years, and in a series of letters to an old friend and fellow diplomat, left a candid and perceptive portrait of the Ottoman world and its aging emperor. The following selection is a portion of a letter he wrote in 1554 recounting his arrival at the Ottoman Court and his impressions of Sultan Suleiman.

TURKISH LETTERS OF OGIER DE BUSBECQ

On our arrival... we were taken to call on Achmet Pasha (the Grand Vizier) and the other pashas- for the Sultan himself was not then in the town- and commenced our negotiations with them touching the business entrusted to us by King Ferdinand. The Pashas, on their part, apparently wishing to avoid any semblance of being prejudiced with regard to these questions, did not offer any strong opposition to the views we expressed, and told us that the whole matter depended on the Sultan's pleasure. On his arrival we were admitted to an audience; but the manner and spirit in which he listened to our address, our arguments, and our message, was by no means favorable.

The Sultan was seated on a very low ottoman, not more than a foot from the ground, which was covered with a quantity of costly rugs and cushions of exquisite workmanship; near him lay his bow and arrows. His air, as I said, was by no means gracious, and his face wore a stern, though dignified, expression.

On entering we were separately conducted into the royal presence by the chamberlains, who grasped our arms.... After having gone through a pretence of kissing his hand, we were conducted backwards to the wall opposite his seat, care being taken that we should never turn our backs on him. The Sultan then listened to what I had to say; but the language I held was not at all to his taste, for the demands of his Majesty breathed a spirit of independence and dignity, which was by no means acceptable to one who deemed that his wish was law; and so he made no answer beyond saying in a tetchy way, "well, well." After this we were dismissed to our quarters....

You will probably wish me to give you my impressions of Solyman.

His years are just beginning to tell on him, but his majestic bearing and indeed his whole demeanour are such as beseem the lord of so vast an empire. He has always had the character of being a careful and temperate man; even in his early days, when, according to the Turkish rule, sin would have been venial, his life was blameless; for not even in youth did he either indulge in wine or commit those unnatural crimes which are common among the Turks; nor could those who were disposed to put the most unfavourable construction on his acts bring anything worse against him than his excessive devotion to his wife, and the precipitate way in which, by her influence he was induced to put Mustapha (his eldest son) to death; for it is commonly believed that it was by her philtres and witchcraft that he was led to commit this act. As regards herself, it is a well-known fact that from the time he made her his lawful wife he has been perfectly faithful to her, although there was nothing in the laws to prevent his having mistresses as well. As an upholder of his religion and its rites he is most strict, being quite as anxious to extend his faith as to extend his empire. Considering his years (for he is now getting on for sixty) he enjoys good health, though it may be that his bad complexion arises form some lurking malady.... When he is anxious to impress an ambassador, who is leaving, with a favourable idea of the state of his health, he conceals the bad complexion of his face under a coat of rouge, his notion being that foreign powers will fear him more if they think that he is strong and well. I detected unmistakable signs of this practice of his; for I observed his face when he gave me a farewell audience, and found it was much altered from what it was when he received me on my arrival....

TEXTUAL QUESTIONS FOR ANALYSIS

1. Why do you think the chamberlains held the arms of De Besbecq when he was admitted to the presence of the Sultan? What does this indicate about the nature of his rule?
2. What appears to impress the ambassador the most about Suleiman? What does he regard as his most negative characteristic?
3. What does the Sultan's use of rouge indicate about the nature of Ottoman government? What is the greatest weakness of such a system?
4. What was the relative balance of power between King Ferdinand and Sultan Suleiman in 1554? Who had the most to gain from a peace treaty?

Source: Ogier Ghiselin de Busbecq, *The Life and Letters of Ogier Ghiselin de Busbecq* (London: Kegan Paul, 1881), pp. 113-120.

CHAPTER 33
AFRICA : FROM COMMERCIAL PARTNER TO COLONY

The Atlantic slave trade reached its peak in the eighteenth century, but this century also saw the beginnings of an anti-slave trade movement in Great Britain, the leading country in the trade. The eighteenth century also witnessed the first concerted efforts by European explorers and traders to penetrate the interior of the continent. These efforts produced the first accurate accounts of the interior of Africa ever published in Western Europe. One of the best of these early accounts is TRAVELS IN THE INTERIOR DISTRICTS OF AFRICA, published in 1797. The author was Mungo Park, a Scottish surgeon, anti-slave trade advocate, and amateur scientist. In 1795 the African Association of England sent him on an expedition to explore the origins of the Niger River. From the mouth of the Gambia River he traveled to the headwaters of the Niger and descended about half its length before being forced to turn back. Aside from his scientific pursuits, he was also interested in studying slavery as it existed in Africa, in hopes of finding some economic alternatives to the slave trade. His book was published upon his return, and offered an eager audience a first-hand account of the interior of West Africa. He returned on a second expedition in 1805, and was drowned in 1806 in the Niger River at the Bussa Rapids. Some of his details and assumptions about West African slavery being typical of the whole continent were later shown to be incorrect, but his account provides valuable information by an interested and sympathetic observer on the practice of slavery in Africa in the late eighteenth century.

TRAVELS IN THE INTERIOR DISTRICTS OF AFRICA

The slaves in Africa, I suppose, are nearly in the proportion of three to one to the freemen. They claim no reward for their services except food and clothing, and are treated with kindness or severity according to the good or bad disposition of their masters. Custom, however, has established certain rules with regard to the treatment of slaves, which it is thought dishonorable to violate. Thus, the domestic slaves, or such as are born in a man's own house, are treated with more leniency than those which are purchased with money. The authority of the master over the domestic slave, as I have elsewhere observed, extends only to reasonable correction: for the master cannot sell his domestic, without having first brought him to a public trial before the chief men of the place.... In time of famine, the master is permitted to sell one or more of his domestics to purchase provisions for his family; and, in case of the master's insolvency, the domestic slaves are sometimes seized upon by his creditors; and if the master cannot redeem them, they are liable to be sold for payment of his debts. These are the only cases that I recollect in which the domestic slaves are liable to be sold, without any misconduct or demerit of their own.

But these restrictions on the power of the master extend not to the case of prisoners taken in war nor to that of slaves purchased with money. All these unfortunate beings are considered as strangers and foreigners, who have no right to the protection of the law, and may be treated with severity or sold to a stranger according to the pleasure of their owners. There are, indeed, regular markets where slaves of this description are bought and sold, and the value of a slave in the eye of an African purchaser increases in proportion to his distance form his native kingdom; for when slaves are only a few days' journey from the place of their nativity, they frequently effect their escape; but when one or more kingdoms intervene, escape being more difficult, they are more readily reconciled to their situation. On this account the unhappy slave is frequently transferred from one dealer to another, until he has lost all hopes of returning to his native kingdom. The slaves which are purchased by the Europeans on the Coast are chiefly of this description; a few of them are collected in petty wars, hereafter to be described, which take place near the Coast, but by far the greater number are brought down in large caravans from the inland countries, of which many are unknown by name to the Europeans. The slaves which are thus brought from the interior may be divided into two distinct classes; first, such as were slaves from their birth, having been born of enslaved mothers; secondly, such as were born free, but who afterward, by whatever means, became slaves. Those of the first description are by far the most numerous; for prisoners taken in war (at least such as are taken in open and declared war, when one kingdom avows hostilities against another) are generally of this description....

Slaves of the second description generally become such by one or other of the following causes: 1. Captivity. 2. Famine. 3. Insolvency. 4. Crimes. A freeman may, by the established customs of Africa, become a slave by being taken in war. War is, of all others, the most productive source, and was probably the origin of slavery.... It is a known fact that prisoners of war in Africa are the slaves of their conquerors; and when the weak or unsuccessful warrior begs for mercy beneath the uplifted spear of his opponent, he gives up at the same time his claim to liberty and purchases his life at the expense of his freedom....

There are many instances of freemen voluntarily surrendering up their liberty to save their lives. During a great famine which lasted for three years in the countries of the Gambia great numbers of people became slaves in this manner.... Large families are very often exposed to absolute want: and, as the parents have almost unlimited authority over their children, it frequently happens, in all parts of Africa, that some of the latter are sold to purchase provisions for the rest of the family....

The third cause of slavery is insolvency. Of all the offenses to which the laws of Africa have affixed the punishment of slavery, this is the most common.... In Africa, not only the effects of the insolvent, but even the insolvent himself, is sold to satisfy the lawful demands of his creditors.

The fourth cause above enumerated is the commission of crimes on which the laws of the country affix slavery as a punishment. In Africa the only offenses of this class are murder, adultery, and witchcraft; and I am happy to say that they did not appear to me to be common....

When a freeman has become a slave by any one of the causes before mentioned, he generally continues so for life, and his children (if they are born to an enslaved mother) are brought up in the same state of servitude....

Such are the general outlines of that system of slavery which prevails in Africa: and it is evident from its nature and extent that it is a system of no modern date. It probably had its origin in the remote ages of antiquity, before the Muslims explored a path across the Desert. How far it is maintained and supported by the slave traffic, which, for two hundred years, the nations of Europe have carried on with the natives of the Coast, it is neither within my province nor in my power to explain. If my sentiments should be required concerning the effect which a discontinuance of that commerce would produce on the manners of the natives, I should have no hesitation in observing that, in the present unenlightened state of their minds, my opinion is that the effect would neither be so extensive or beneficial, as many wise and worthy persons fondly expect.

TEXTUAL QUESTIONS FOR ANALYSIS

1. What appear to be the most important differences between African slavery and the enslavement of Africans in the European colonies of the Americas? What are the similarities?
2. What are the different types of slavery that Park found in West Africa, and did certain slaves have more rights and privileges than others?
3. As an opponent of the Atlantic slave trade do you think Park was encouraged or discouraged by what he found on his travels? Explain.
4. What are the ways in which one could become a slave in Africa? Which is most likely, and which is least likely? What is the origin of most the slaves of the coastal trade?

Source: Mungo Park, *Travels in the Interior Districts of Africa* (London: 1799), pp. 318-320, 331-332).

CHAPTER 34
LATIN AMERICA FROM COLONY TO DEPENDENT STATEHOOD

Simon Bolivar (1783-1830) was the greatest of the Latin American revolutionary leaders of the early nineteenth century and is known even today as "El Libertador." His father was a wealthy Venezuelan nobleman, and young Bolivar received all the benefits that wealth and position could provide. After the death of his parents, he traveled to Spain to complete his education and to find a suitable wife. He returned to Venezuela in 1807 after Napoleon's conquest of Spain, and became involved in the early movements for independence offered by the French occupation of Spain. In 1811 Venezuela declared its independence, beginning a revolutionary struggle that would last until 1822. Bolivar became a leading figure in the war for independence, enduring frequent defeats (1812 and 1815), and even a brief period of exile in Jamaica in 1815. It was during this period of exile that he composed one of his most famous political statements, THE JAMAICAN LETTER. It was intended as an appeal for support from those Latin American aristocrats not yet committed to the revolution, and as encouragement for his supporters and fellow revolutionaries at a low point in the struggle against Spain. By this time it was clear that neither Europe nor the United States were going to offer active assistance against Spain, so Bolivar issued an optimistic assessment of the situation and predicted eventual success through Latin Americans' own efforts. He also offered ideas about the future organization of the various states of South America, ideas which he attempted to put into practice after independence when he became president of Peru, Colombia, and Bolivia.

THE JAMAICAN LETTER

It is difficult to foresee the future state of the New World, to set down its political principles, or to prophesy what manner of government it will adopt. Every conjecture relative to America's future is, I feel, pure speculation.... We are a young people. We inhabit a world apart, separated by broad seas. We are young in the ways of almost all the arts and sciences, although, in a certain manner, we are old in the ways of civilized society. I look upon the present state of America as similar to that of Rome after its fall. Each part of Rome adopted a political system conforming to its interest and situation or was led by the individual ambitions of certain chiefs, dynasties, or associations. But this important difference exists: those dispersed parts later re-established their ancient nations, subject to the changes imposed by circumstances or events. But we scarcely retain a vestige of what once was; we are, moreover, neither Indian nor European, but a species midway between the legitimate proprietors of this country and the Spanish usurpers. In short, though Americans by birth we derive our rights from Europe, and we have to assert these rights against the rights of the natives, and at the same time we must defend ourselves against the invaders. This places us in a most extraordinary and involved situation....

The role of the inhabitants of the American hemisphere has for centuries been purely passive. Politically they were non-existent. We are still in a position lower than slavery, and therefore it is more difficult for us to rise to the enjoyment of freedom.... We have been harassed by a conduct which has not only deprived us of our rights but has kept us in a sort of permanent infancy with regard to public affairs. If we could at least have managed our domestic affairs and our internal administration, we could have acquainted ourselves with the processes and mechanics of public affairs. We should also have enjoyed a personal consideration, thereby commanding a certain unconscious respect from the people, which is so necessary to preserve amidst revolutions. That is why I say we have even been deprived of an active tyranny, since we have not been permitted to exercise its functions.

Americans today, and perhaps to a greater extent than ever before, who live within the Spanish system occupy a position in society no better than that of serfs destined for labor, or at best they have no more status than that of mere consumers. Yet even this status is surrounded with galling restrictions, such as being forbidden to grow European crops, or to store products which are royal monopolies, or to establish factories of a type the Peninsula itself does not possess. To this add the exclusive trading privileges, even in articles of prime necessity, and the barriers between American provinces, designed to prevent all exchange of trade, traffic, and understanding. In short, do you wish to know what our future held?- simply the cultivation of the fields of indigo, grain, coffee, sugar cane, cacao, and cotton; cattle raising on the broad plains; hunting wild game in the jungles; digging in the earth to mine its gold- but even these limitations could never satisfy the greed of Spain....

More than anyone, I desire to see America fashioned into the greatest nation in the world, greatest not so much by virtue of her area and wealth as by her freedom and glory. Although I seek perfection for the government of my country, I cannot persuade myself that the New World can, at the moment, be organized as a great republic. Since it is impossible, I dare not desire it; yet much less do I desire to have all America a monarchy because this plan is not only impracticable but also impossible. Wrongs now existing could not be righted, and our emancipation would be fruitless. The American states need the care of paternal governments to heal the sores and wounds of despotism and war....

Among the popular and representative systems, I do not favor the federal system. It is overperfect, and it demands political virtues and talents far superior to our own. For the same reason I reject a monarchy that is part aristocracy and part democracy, although with such a government England has achieved much fortune and splendor. Since it is not possible for us to select the most perfect and complete form of government, let us avoid falling into demagogic anarchy or monocratic tyranny. These opposite extremes would only wreck us on similar reefs of misfortune and dishonor; hence, we must seek a mean between them. I say: Do not adopt the best system of government, but the one that is most likely to succeed.

TEXTUAL QUESTIONS FOR ANALYSIS

1. According to Bolivar, what have been the worst aspects of Spain's rule, and what are the chief grievances against the Spanish?
2. Do you see any similarities between his list of Spain's misdeeds and the complaints of the North American revolutionaries against the British? Be specific.
3. What type of government does he apparently think will work best after independence? Does he apparently assume that there will be several separate countries or one large state? Why?
4. Compare this political manifesto to that of Madison in the Federalist Papers in Chapter 36. Which is more sophisticated and why?

Source: Harold A. Bierck, ed., and Lewis Berrand, trans., *Simon Bolivar, Selected Writings* (New York: Colonial Press, 1951), pp. 103-110.

CHAPTER 35
THE SCIENTIFIC REVOLUTION AND ITS ENLIGHTENED AFTERMATH

John Locke (1632-1704) was both a political philosopher and the founder of modern empiricism. Educated at Oxford, he was not only a scholar, but also a doctor, a civil servant, and an amateur diplomat. A supporter and propagandist for Parliament against the power of the crown, he was sent into exile in Holland from 1682 to 1688. He returned with the fleet that brought William and Mary to England, and soon produced his best known political work, A TREATISE ON CIVIL GOVERNMENT, in which he presented a theoretical justification for the victory of Parliament over James II. But his chief claim to fame rests on his philosophical writings, the most important of which is AN ESSAY CONCERNING HUMAN UNDERSTANDING. He is regarded as one of the leading figures of the Enlightenment because his theories became widely accepted and provided justification for the concept of human perfectibility that was such a distinguishing feature of Enlightenment thought. Traditional Christian doctrine pictured man as a fallen creature, destined for sin and damnation without the grace of God. Traditional ideas of learning held that all important knowledge was inborn, so education was mainly a process of remembering what was already there, but had not yet been uncovered. Locke offered a radically different concept, and began the nature versus nurture debate that is still with us. He asserted that all of our knowledge, including concepts of right and wrong, come from sense experience organized by the mind. Thus, people were not born bad or sinful, they learned to become bad or sinful through their experiences. Change those experiences and you could change human nature. Good environments could and would produce better people. It was a radically new idea and opened up new concepts of human progress.

AN ESSAY CONCERNING HUMAN UNDERSTANDING

It is an established opinion amongst some men that there are in the understanding certain innate principles; some primary notions,.... characters, as it were, stamped upon the mind of man; which the soul receives in its very first being, and brings into the world with it. It would be sufficient to convince unprejudiced readers of the falseness of this supposition, if I should only show (as I hope I shall in the following parts of this Discourse) how men, barely by the use of their natural faculties, may attain to all the knowledge they have, without the help of any innate impressions; and may arrive at certainty, without any such original notions or principles....

Let us suppose the mind to be, as we say, white paper, void of all characters, without any ideas:- How comes it to be furnished? Whence comes it by that vast store which the busy and boundless fancy of man has painted on it with an almost endless variety? Whence has it all materials of reason and knowledge? To this I answer, in one word, from EXPERIENCE. In that all our knowledge is founded; and from that it ultimately derives itself. Our observation employed either, about external sensible objects, or about the internal operations of our minds perceived and reflected on by ourselves, is that which supplies our understandings with all the materials of thinking. These two are the foundations of knowledge, from whence all the ideas we have, or can naturally have, do spring....

FAITH AND REASON

By what has been said of reason, we may be able to make some guess at the distinction of things, into those that are according to, above, and contrary to reason. (1) According to reason are such propositions whose truth we can discover by examining and tracing those ideas we have from sensation and reflection; and by natural deduction find to be true or probable. (2) Above reason are such propositions whose truth or probability we cannot by reason derive from those principles. (3) Contrary to reason are such propositions as are inconsistent with or irreconcilable to our clear and distinct ideas. Thus the existence of one God is according to reason; the existence of more than one God, contrary to reason; the resurrection of the dead, above reason....

There is another use of the word reason, wherein it is opposed to faith.... Only I think it may not be amiss to take notice, that, however faith be opposed to reason, faith is nothing but a firm assent of the mind: which, if it be regulated, as is our duty, cannot be afforded to anything but upon good reason; and so cannot be opposite to it. He that believes without having any reason for believing, may be in love with his own fancies; but neither seeks truth as he ought, nor pays the obedience due to his Maker, who would have him use those discerning faculties he has given him, to keep him out of mistake and error....

TEXTUAL QUESTIONS FOR ANALYSIS

1. Why was Locke's approach to knowledge favorable toward the encouragement of scientific experimentation?
2. How would the views of Locke promote the concept of religious toleration?
3. What would be a Lockean approach toward criminal behavior? Why?
4. How did Locke define "reason," and what was the role of reason in questions of religious dogma? Is Locke anti-religion, pro-religion, or neither? Explain.

Source: A. C. Fraser, ed., *John Locke, An Essay Concerning Human Understanding* (Oxford: The Clarendon Press, 1894), Vol. 1, pp. 37-38, 121-122.

CHAPTER 36
LIBERALISM AND THE CHALLENGE TO ABSOLUTIST MONARCHY

Liberalism of the modern variety was born in the eighteenth century Enlightenment, and its ideals are expressed eloquently in the American Declaration of Independence and the French Declaration of the Rights of Man. But the first national government to be organized and based on such principles was the one created by the Constitution of the United States. The debates over the Constitution and its ratification produced some of the best political writing of the era, and are still considered models of lucidity. THE FEDERALIST is the title given to a series of articles written by Alexander Hamilton and John Jay of New York, and James Madison of Virginia in 1787 and 1788 that attempted to defend the Constitution and promote its ratification. The Constitution was completed by the Constitutional Convention in Philadelphia in September, 1787, and the debate over its ratification by the thirteen separate states was quite intense. The articles appeared anonymously in the newspapers of New York City, and were intended to help insure ratification by the state of New York. They were quickly reprinted in other states, and after ratification was successful, the authors revealed themselves and allowed publication of the complete series. The following selection, Number 51, was written by James Madison, and attempts to answer the question of how the new government, organized under the new constitution, will deal with the age-old political problem of how to prevent a powerful government from becoming too powerful, and thus abridging the freedoms it was created to protect.

THE FEDERALIST, NUMBER 51

To what expedient then shall we finally resort, for maintaining in practice the necessary partition of power among the several departments, as laid down in the constitution? The only answer that can be given is, that as all these exterior provisions are found to be inadequate, the defect must be supplied, by so contriving the interior structure of the government, as that its several constituent parts may, by their mutual relations, be the means of keeping each other in their proper places. Without presuming to undertake a full development of this important idea, I will hazard a few general observations, which may, perhaps, place it in a clearer light, and enable us to form a more correct judgment of the principles and structure of the government planned by the convention.

In order to lay a due foundation for that separate and distinct exercise of the different powers of government, which, to a certain extent, is admitted on all hands to be essential to the preservation of liberty, it is evident that each department should have a will of its own; and consequently should be so constituted, that the members of each should have as little agency as possible in the appointment of the members of the others....

It is equally evident, that the members of each department should be as little dependent as possible on those of the others, for the emoluments annexed to their offices. Were the executive magistrate, or the judges, not independent of the legislature in this particular, their independence in every other, would be merely nominal.

But the great security against a gradual concentration of the several powers in the same department, consists in giving to those who administer each department, the necessary constitutional means, and personal motives, to resist encroachments of the others. The provision for defence must in this, as in all other cases, be made commensurate to the danger of attack. Ambition must be made to counteract ambition. The interest of the man must be connected with the constitutional rights of the place. It may be a reflection on human nature, that such devices should be necessary to control the abuses of government. But what is government itself, but the greatest of all reflections on human nature? If men were angels, no government would be necessary. If angels were to govern men, neither external nor internal controls on government would be necessary. In framing a government, which is to be administered by men over men, the great difficulty lies in this: You must first enable the government to control the governed; and in the next place, oblige it to control itself. A dependence on the people is, no doubt, the primary control on the government; but experience has taught mankind the necessity of auxiliary precautions....

TEXTUAL QUESTIONS FOR ANALYSIS

1. According to Madison how are the rights of the people to be protected in this new government and what is the safeguard against the concentration of power?
2. Describe specific examples from the political situation of today that show how Madison's concept is still working.
3. Although based on liberal theory as to the purpose and basis of government, what is the basis for the actual working of the system described by Madison?
4. What is the difference between the governmental system described by Bishop Bossuet (Chapter 30) and Madison? Be specific.

Source: Richard W. Lyman and Lewis W. Spitz, eds., *Major Crisis in Western Civilization*, (New York: Harcourt Brace and World, 1965), Vol. 1, pp. 71-72.

CHAPTER 37
THE FRENCH REVOLUTION AND THE BONAPARTIST EMPIRE

The French Revolution began as an attempt by liberal delegates from the Third Estate to establish a constitutional monarchy, based on equality under the law, similar to the system prevailing in England. Within a few years after the destruction of absolute monarchy, France had become a radical republic, advocating the overthrow of monarchy throughout Europe, and enforcing obedience at home through a system of brutal political repression known as the Reign of Terror. A few years later a new ruler, Napoleon Bonaparte, had restored order and become the first modern dictator, with power and authority far beyond any ever possessed by Louis XIV.

Unlike the American Revolution, the French Revolution attracted international opposition from the very beginning, as absolute monarchs throughout Europe looked with fear upon the events in France from 1789-1792. By the spring of 1792, France was at war with Prussia and the Austrian Empire, and middle class revolutionaries lost control of events as the war radicalized and accelerated the process of change. The war went badly for the French at first, and Louis XVI tried to flee the country. Faced with a monarch who was an enemy to the concept of constitutional government, and defeat on the battlefield, the moderates lost control of the revolutionary government, and a republic was proclaimed. The radical Jacobin party, led by Robespierre, instituted a Reign of Terror as a way of enforcing loyalty to the new republic, and dealing with the threat of counter-revolution. The following selection is the speech made by Robespierre to the National Convention on February 5, 1794, in which he presented the aims of the revolution as he envisioned them, and justified the Terror.

ROBESPIERRE'S SPEECH TO THE NATIONAL CONVENTION

What is the aim we want to achieve? The peaceful enjoyment of liberty and equality, the reign of that eternal justice whose laws have been engraved, not in stone and marble, but in the hearts of all men, even in the heart of the slave who forgets them or of the tyrant who denies them.

We want a state of affairs where all despicable and cruel passions are unknown and all kind and generous passions are aroused by the laws; when ambition is the desire to deserve glory and to serve the fatherland; where decisions arise only from equality itself; where the citizen submits to the magistrate, the magistrate to the people and the people to justice; where the fatherland guarantees the well-being of each individual, and where each individual enjoys with pride the prosperity and the glory of the fatherland; where all souls elevate themselves through constant communication of republican sentiments and through the need to deserve the esteem of a great people; where the arts are the decorations of liberty that ennobles them, where commerce is the source of public wealth and not only of the monstrous opulence of a few houses.

In our country we want to substitute morality for egoism, honesty for honor, principles for customs, duties for decorum, the rule of reason for the tyranny of custom, the contempt of vice for the contempt of misfortune, pride for insolence, magnanimity for vanity, love of glory for the love of money, good people for well-bred people, merit for intrigue, genius for wit, truth for pompous action,.... all the virtues and all the miracles of the Republic for all the vices and all the absurdities of the monarchy.

In one word, we want to fulfill the wishes of nature, accomplish the destiny of humanity, keep the promises of philosophy, absolve Providence from the long reign of crime and tyranny.

What kind of government can realize these marvels? Only a democratic or republican government.

But what is the fundamental principle of the democratic or popular government, that is to say, the essential strength that sustains it and makes it move? It is virtue: I am speaking of the public virtue which brought about so many marvels in Greece and Rome and which must bring about much more astonishing ones yet in republican France; of that virtue which is nothing more than love of fatherland and of its laws.

If the strength of popular government in peacetime is virtue, the strength of popular government in revolution is both virtue and terror; terror without virtue is disastrous, virtue without terror is powerless. Terror is nothing but prompt, severe, inflexible justice; it is thus an emanation of virtue; it is less a particular principle than a consequence of the general principle of democracy applied to the most urgent needs of the fatherland. It is said that terror is the strength of despotic government. Does ours resemble despotism? Yes, as the sword that shines in the hands of the heroes of liberty resemble the one with which the satellites of tyranny are armed. Let the despot govern his brutalized subjects through terror; he is right as a despot. Subdue the enemies of liberty through terror and you will be right as the founders of the Republic. The government of revolution is the despotism of liberty against tyranny.

TEXTUAL QUESTIONS FOR ANALYSIS

1. According to Robespierre, what are the goals of the republic? Are these goals that appear appropriate for a democracy?
2. What is the contradiction between his goals and the means he proposes for accomplishing these goals?
3. Are there revolutionary movements in the world today that espouse similar goals? What about their means?
4. Why is Robespierre's downfall and death not surprising?

Source: Brian Tierney and Joan Scott, eds., *Western Societies: A Documentary History* (New York: Alfred Knopf, 1984), Vol. 2, pp. 222-225.

CHAPTER 38
EUROPE'S INDUSTRIALIZATION

As your text points out, England led the way in early industrialization. The most conspicuous feature of this method of production was the factory system, which utilized machine production and meant bringing large numbers of workers together. The old handicraft system of production had been characterized by small workshops scattered throughout rural villages, often run by extended families, and workers establishing their own pace and scale of production. But the new machines, which were capable of enormous output, were too expensive and needed far more energy for their operation than could supplied by muscle power alone. Thus, machines had to be grouped together for economic and technological reasons, and this meant that the workers would have to be concentrated as well. These early factories were soon notable for their filthiness, unsafe operating conditions, and uncontrolled human exploitation, as factory owners attempted to maximize profits in a business environment characterized by cutthroat competition, and unregulated growth. One of the great scandals of these early factories, especially in the textile industry, was their heavy reliance on child labor. Humanitarian reformers, some of them leading members of English society, pushed for some type of protection for these children, many of them orphans, and this led to the appointment in 1832 of a Parliamentary committee to investigate working conditions in English textile factories. Known as the Sadler Committee, after its Parliamentary chairman Michael Sadler, it held public hearings for several months and then published its findings, along with the evidence given by workers and managers who had testified. The report provided the basis for the first factory worker protection law ever enacted, the 1833 Factory Act, which banned children under nine from factory employment, established a 48 hour maximum work week for children from nine to thirteen, a 68 hour week for those children from thirteen to eighteen, and required part-time schooling for factory children under thirteen. This may not seem like much protection by modern standards, but it was the first time any government in Europe had attempted to regulate conditions of labor, and the length of labor allowed for children under the law provides some indication of how bad conditions were before its passage. The following selection is part of the evidence provided to the committee by Elizabeth Bentley, a 23 year old textile worker from the factory town of Leeds who had been sent to work in the mills at age six. Her recollections provide a vivid picture of the human cost of early industrialization.

THE SADLER REPORT, 1832

Bentley, Elizabeth, age 23- examined, 4th June, 1832,- as doffer, began to work, when six years old, in a flax mill, Leeds.
1. What were your hours of labour? - From five in the morning, till nine at night, when they were thronged.
2. For how long a time together have you worked that excessive length of time? - For about half a year.

3. What were your usual hours of labour, when you were not thronged? - From six in the morning, till seven at night.
4. What time was allowed for your meals? - Forty minutes, at noon.
5. Had you any time to get your breakfast, or drinking? - No, we got it as we could.
6. And when your work was bad, you had hardly any time to eat it at all? - No; we were obliged to leave it or to take it home, and when we did not take it, the overlooker took it, and gave it to his pigs.
7. Do you consider doffing a laborious employment? - Yes; when the frames are full, they have to stop the frames, and take the flyers off, and take the full bobbins off, and carry them to the roller, and then put empty ones on, and set the frames going again.
8. Does that keep you constantly on your feet? - Yes; there are so many frames, and they run so quick.
9. Suppose you flagged a little, or were too late, what would they do? - Strap us.
10. Girls as well as boys? - Yes.
11. Have you ever been strapped? - Yes, severely.
12. Were you strapped if you were too much fatigued to keep up with the machinery? - Yes; the overlooker I was under was a very severe man, and when we have been fatigued, and worn out, and had not baskets to put the bobbins in, we used to put them in the window bottoms, and that broke the panes sometimes, and I broke one time, and the overlooker strapped me on the arm, and it rose a blister, and I ran home to my mother.
13. How long were you in your first situation? - Three or four years.
14. Where did you go then? - To Benyon's factory.
15. What were you there? - A weigher in the card-room.
16. How long did you work there? - From half-past five, till eight at night.
17. The carding-room is more oppressive than the spinning department? - Yes, it is so dusty; they cannot see each other for dust.
18. Did working in the card-room affect your health? - Yes; it was so dusty, the dust got up my lungs, and the work was so hard; I was middling strong when I went there, but the work was so bad; I got so bad in health, that when I pulled the baskets down, I pulled my bones out of their places.
19. You are considerably deformed in your person in consequence of this labour? - Yes, I am.
20. At what time did it come on? - I was about thirteen years old when it began coming, and it has got worse since; it is five years since my mother died, and my mother was never able to get me a pair of stays to hold me up; when my mother died, I had to do for myself, and got me a pair.
21. Were you straight till you were thirteen? - Yes, I was.
22. Have you been attended to by any medical gentleman at Leeds, or the neighbourhood? - Yes, I have been under Mr. Hares.
23. To what did he attribute it? - He said it was owing to hard labour, and working in the factories.
24. Where are you now? - In the poor house.
25. Do any of your former employers come to see you? - No.
26. Did you ever receive anything from them when you became afflicted? - When I was at home, Mr. Walker made me a present of one or two shillings; but since I have left my work and gone to the poor house, they have not come nigh me.
27. You are supported by the parish? - Yes.

28. You are utterly incapable now of any exertion in the factories? - Yes.
29. You were very willing to have worked as long as you were able, from your earliest age? - Yes.
30. And to have supported your widowed mother as long as you could? - Yes....

TEXTUAL QUESTIONS FOR ANALYSIS

1. Based on the information contained in her evidence, what assumptions can be made about Elizabeth Bentley's life story up to age 23? What about her future prospects?
2. Based on her testimony, how many hours a week was she working at age six during busy periods and normal periods, excluding Sundays when the factory was closed? What evidence is there relative to her education? What is the significance of this?
3. Based on modern knowledge of maturation and nutrition, what do you think happened to Elizabeth Bentley at age thirteen? What responsibility did her employers assume?
4. Would the Factory Act of 1833 have helped Elizabeth Bentley had it been in effect when she began to work in the mill? How?

Source: *Report from the Committee on the Bill to Regulate the Labour of Children in the Mills and the Factories of the United Kingdom* (London: British Sessional Papers, 1832), Vol. 15, pp. 195-198.

CHAPTER 39
THE SOCIAL IMPACTS OF EARLY INDUSTRY

The rapid growth of cities was one of the most obvious results of early industrialization. The rate of population growth dramatically accelerated in the early nineteenth century throughout Europe, but the rate of urban growth was even more phenomenal. Cities grew not only because of rising population levels, but primarily due to the spread of the factory system. Workers were drawn from the countryside to the cities for the new factory jobs. The pay was low and the working conditions were a scandal, but factory work promised cash wages and the lure of the big city. But this rapid urban growth, especially in England, was unregulated and unrestrained. England had no experience with urban growth of such scale and rapidity. The city of Manchester had less than 20,000 people in 1800, and by 1831 there were 142,000. In 1801 when England conducted its first national census, there were only thirteen towns with populations over 20,000; by 1891 there were sixty-three. In early nineteenth century England, there were no zoning laws, no building codes, no regulations relative to sewage disposal, and no governmental regulations regarding the supply of fresh water. As cities grew rapidly, the results were predictable. Crowded, shabbily constructed housing, and unsanitary conditions for waste disposal and the supply of water led to frequent outbreaks of diseases such as typhoid and cholera. The germ theory of disease was still fifty years in the future in the 1830's, but medical authorities did realize that there was a connection between cleanliness and health. These grim conditions led to Parliamentary investigations of the living conditions of the new industrial cities, and the ultimate result was the adoption of sanitary regulations relative to sewage and fresh water, zoning codes, and building regulations. By the late nineteenth century the urban environment of England was much cleaner and healthier. The following selection is a description of the sanitary conditions of Manchester in 1840 written by a Dr. John Robertson as part of his evidence for a parliamentary commission investigating the living conditions of England's industrial cities. The purpose of the 1840 investigation was to see if local governments needed more power to regulate and control the unbridled growth that was taking place.

THE CONDITION OF MANCHESTER, 1840

Until twelve years ago there was no paving and sewering Act in any of the townships; even in the township of Manchester, containing in the year 1831 upwards of 142,000 inhabitants, this was the case; and the disgraceful condition of the streets and sewers on the invasion of cholera you have no doubt learned from Dr. Kay's able and valuable pamphlet. At the present time the paving of the streets proceeds rapidly in every direction, and great attention is given to the drains. Upon the whole, it is gratifying to bear testimony to the zeal of the authorities in carrying on the salutary improvements, especially when it is known that no street can be paved or sewered without the consent of the owners of property, unless a certain large proportion of the land on either side is built upon. Owing to this cause several important streets remain to this hour disgraceful nuisances.

Manchester has no Building Act, and hence, with the exception of certain central streets, over which the Police Act gives the Commissioners power, each proprietor builds as he pleases. New cottages, with or without cellars, huddled together row behind row, may be seen springing up in many parts, but especially in the township of Manchester, where the land is higher in price than the land for cottage sites in other townships. With such proceedings as these the authorities cannot interfere. A cottage row may be badly drained, the streets may be full of pits, brimful of stagnant water, the receptacle of dead cats and dogs, yet no one may find fault. The number of cellar residences, you have probably learned from the papers published by the Manchester Statistical Society, is very great in all quarters of the town;.... That it is an evil must be obvious on the slightest consideration, for how can a hole underground of from 12 to 15 feet square admit of ventilation so as to fit it for a human habitation.

We have no authorized inspector of dwellings and streets. If an epidemic disease were to invade, as happened in 1832, the authorities would probably order inspection, as they did on that occasion, but it would be merely by general permission, not of right.

So long as this and other great manufacturing towns were multiplying and extending their branches of manufacture and were prosperous, every fresh addition of operatives found employment, good wages, and plenty of food; and so long as the families of working people are well fed, it is certain they maintain their health in a surprising manner, even in cellars or other close dwellings. Now, however, the case is different. Food is dear, labour scarce, and wages in many branches very low; consequently, as might be expected, disease and death are making unusual havoc. In the years 1833, 1834, 1835, and 1836 (years of prosperity), the number of fever cases admitted into the Manchester House of Recovery amounted to only 1,685, or 421 per annum; while in the two pinching years, 1838 and 1839, the number admitted was 2, 414, or 1,207 per annum. It is in such a depressed state of the manufacturing districts as at present exists that unpaved and badly sewered streets, narrow alleys, close, unventilated courts and cellars, exhibit their malign influence in augmenting the sufferings which that greatest of all physical evils, want of sufficient food, inflicts on young and old in large towns, but especially on the young.

Manchester has no public park or other grounds where the population can walk and breathe the fresh air. New streets are rapidly extending in every direction, and so great already is the expanse of the town, that those who live in the more populous quarters can seldom hope to see the green face of nature.... In this respect Manchester is disgracefully defective; more so, perhaps, than any other town in the empire. Every advantage of this nature has been sacrificed to the getting of money in the shape of ground-rents.

TEXTUAL QUESTIONS FOR ANALYSIS

1. To what does the doctor attribute the unhealthy living conditions of Manchester- a conspiracy by industrialists, lack of government authority, the desire of landowners to maximize profits and rents, the ignorance of the working class, or a combination of some of these. Explain.
2. In what ways do the living conditions of early nineteenth century Manchester resemble and differ from those of rapidly growing cities in developing countries today?
3. How did England's capitalist system contribute to the poor living conditions of the working class in Manchester?
4. What would Dr. Robertson like to see happen in order to make Manchester a better place to live?

Source: John Saville, ed., *Working Conditions in the Victorian Age* (Westmead, England: Gregg International Publishers, Ltd., 1973), pp. 130-132.

CHAPTER 40
EUROPE IN IDEOLOGICAL CONFLICT

Nationalism was one of the great legacies of the French Revolution. It was a revolutionary doctrine, and inherently hostile to the conservative monarchies and empires that continued to dominate most of Europe after the Congress of Vienna. The central concept of nationalism was that each separate "nation" had an undeniable and inherent "right" of separate nationhood. Thus, dynastic states like Austria or Russia, in which all types of different "nations" were ruled by foreign monarchs were considered unacceptable and tyrannical. The solution of the nationalists was a revolution of the oppressed peoples in which foreign tyranny would be overthrown, and republican and truly national governments would be established based on the consent of the people. The enemies of the nationalists were the multinational dynastic monarchies, such as the Austrian Empire, the nobility whose status was based on inherited privileges, and the Roman Catholic Church, which was a bastion of anti-republican and anti-nationalist sentiment, and thus allied with the existing conservative regimes.

Italy after 1815 was divided between small monarchies in the northern half of the peninsula that were under the control of the Austrian Empire, a central portion of small states under the direct control of the Papacy, and the southern pro-Austrian Kingdom of the Two Sicilies. Such a situation of foreign direct and indirect rule was a fertile ground for nationalism, and in 1820, 1830, and 1848 there were nationalist revolutions in Italy that attempted to drive out the Austrians and their allies and establish an Italian republic. The man who became the greatest prophet of nineteenth century Italian nationalism was Joseph Mazzini (1805-1872), the son of a well-respected doctor of the northern city of Genoa. Mazzini was a typical mid-nineteenth century anticlerical liberal nationalist who spent his life preaching the doctrine of a unified and indivisible Italian republic. He wanted all Italians unified under a secular, peaceful republic that would serve as a beacon to other oppressed peoples. His greatest moment of glory came when he was elected to head the short-lived Roman Republic of 1848. But the republic was crushed by French and Austrian troops, and Mazzini spent most of the remainder of his life in exile, attempting to develop a sense of Italian nationalism among the masses through his propaganda, and plotting new revolts to overthrow Austrian rule in Italy. The following selection is from his autobiography, and contains his account of his youthful conversion to nationalism. Notice the almost religious tone of the account as he recounts how he first felt the stirrings of nationalist sentiments as a sixteen-year-old boy, and decided on his life's vocation. The event that he is describing was the short and unsuccessful nationalist revolt of 1820 in the small northern Italian kingdom of Piedmont which was crushed by Austrian and Piedmontese troops.

MAZZINI'S CONVERSION TO NATIONALISM

One Sunday in April 1821, while I was yet a boy, I was walking in the Strada Nuova of Genoa with my mother, and an old friend of our family named Andrea Gambini. The Piedmontese insurrection had just been crushed; partly by Austria, partly through treachery, and partly through the weakness of its leaders.

The revolutionists, seeking safety by sea, had flocked to Genoa, and, finding themselves distressed for means, they went about seeking help to enable them to cross into Spain, where the revolution was yet triumphant. The greater number of them were crowded in S. Pier d'Arena, waiting a chance to embark; but not a few had contrived to enter the city one by one, and I used to search them out from amongst our own people, detecting them either by their general appearance, by some peculiarity of dress, by their warlike air, or by the signs of a deep and silent sorrow on their faces....

Presently we were stopped and addressed by a tall black-bearded man, with a severe and energetic countenance, and a fiery glance that I have never since forgotten. He held out a white handkerchief toward us, merely saying, for the refugees of Italy. My mother and friend dropped some money into the handkerchief, and he turned from us to put the same request to others. I afterwards learned his name. He was one Rini, a captain in the National Guard, which had been instituted at the commencement of the movement. He accompanied those for whom he had thus constituted himself collector, and, I believe, died- as so many of ours have perished- for the cause of liberty in Spain.

That day was the first in which a confused idea presented itself to my mind- I will not say of country, or of liberty- but an idea that we Italians could and therefore ought to struggle for the liberty of our country. I had already been unconsciously educated in the worship of equality by the democratic principles of my parents, whose bearing toward high or low was ever the same. Whatever the position of the individual, they simply regarded the man and sought only the honest man. And my own natural aspirations towards liberty were fostered by constantly hearing my father and the friend already mentioned speak of the recent republican era in France; by the study of the works of Livy and Tacitus, which my Latin master had given me to translate; and by certain old French newspapers, which I discovered half-hidden behind my father's medical books. Amongst these last were some numbers.... of a Girondist publication belonging to the first period of the French Revolution.

But the idea of an existing wrong in my own country, against which it was a duty to struggle, and the thought that I too must bear my part in that struggle, flashed before my mind on that day for the first time, never again to leave me. The remembrance of those refugees, many of whom became my friends in after life, pursued me wherever I went by day, and mingled with my dreams by night. I would have given I know not what to follow them. I began collecting names and facts, and studied, as best I might, the records of that heroic struggle, seeking to fathom the causes of its failure.

They had been betrayed and abandoned by those who had sworn to concentrate every effort in the movement; the new king (Carlo Felice) had invoked the aid of Austria; part of the Piedmontese troops had even preceded the Austrians.... and the leaders had allowed themselves to be overwhelmed at the first encounter, without making an effort to resist. All the details I succeeded in collecting led me to think that they might have conquered, if all of them had done their duty; then why not renew the attempt?

This idea ever took stronger possession of my soul, and my spirit was crushed by the impossibility I then felt of even conceiving by what means to reduce it to action. Upon the benches of the University....in the midst of the noisy tumultuous life of the students around me, I was sombre and absorbed, and appeared like one suddenly grown old. I childishly determined to dress always in black, fancying myself in mourning for my country.... Matters went so far that my poor mother became terrified lest I should commit suicide.

TEXTUAL QUESTIONS FOR ANALYSIS

1. What role did his parents play in the nationalist conversion of the young Mazzini? Why would his father have hidden his old French newspapers?
2. How and in what way does this account resemble a religious conversion?
3. Why would Mazzini have been opposed to the Papacy?
4. What are the resemblances and differences between Mazzini's nationalism and the nationalisms found today in various parts of the world still undergoing nationalist struggles?

Source: Ella Noyes, trans., *Joseph Mazzini, The Duties of Man* (London: J. M. Dent and Sons, Ltd., 1907), pp. 51-53.

CHAPTER 41
CONSOLIDATION OF NATIONAL STATES

The period 1850-1871 witnessed the height of national unification in Europe as first Italy, and then Germany, became unified nation states. But these successful unification campaigns were not the fulfillment of liberal constitutional plans; they were brought by diplomatic agreements among the major powers and successful international wars. It was power politics backed up by military might that created these new nations and changed permanently the balance of power in Europe. Italy had not been a unified state since the fall of the Roman Empire, and Germany had been only a geographic term, not a nation, since the eleventh century. The great diplomatic question of the day was how the new states would conduct their international affairs?

The Franco-Prussian War of 1870-71 resulted in the unification of Germany under Prussian leadership, but it also proved to be a very costly war in human and economic terms and a source of rankling humiliation for France. One of the few bright moments for the French army was the siege of the fortifications of Belfort Castle in eastern France. In spite of intensive attacks and bombardment, the Castle held out for three months (November 2, 1870 - February 13, 1871) against the Germans. But there was a high human cost to this effort at national unification, and the following excerpts from the diary of a young French girl whose father was a member of the Belfort garrison clearly indicate the reality behind the slogans of the politicians of the day. The glorious resistance praised by French military leaders was anything but glorious, and one may see foreshadowed in her diary entries the horrific scenes of trench warfare that were to unfold in World War I.

INSIDE BELFORT CASTLE, 1870-1871

Saturday, 9 December:....As I write these lines, at 8 P.M., the enemy bombardment is intense. Shells whistle as they pass over our heads and explode all around us. Papa (a non-commissioned officer in the French army) is out there constantly, and we are very worried about him. It is sheer torment.
Night of December 11: ....At midnight a shell landed near the opening of our casement, but fortunately failed to explode....
12 December: A great many town buildings were shelled once again....People who have lost their shelter seek refuge in the basements of the town hall and the church. They are tightly packed together. The air is foul; men, women, and children are bunched together and sanitation is totally lacking....
Night of December 14-15: A shell hit the home of Mr. Touvet, cloth-merchant, killed his daughter, and caused a great deal of damage. Mr. Touvet paid four stretcher-bearers 20 francs to take her body to the hospital morgue, and, while he was there mourning, they returned to his house and stole all that had not been destroyed by the explosion. Mr. Touvet lost everything on that same day.

20 December: The shelling never stops!.... Streets are covered with debris. Papa ran back to what remained of our town house to find provisions. While returning, two shells exploded near him and knocked him down. A pot of string beans was broken and scattered, his basket was totally crushed, two bottles of wine smashed, and pears squashed all over the street. He came back looking as black as a chimney-sweep. But he insisted on going back again with a towel, and retrieving his precious string beans, which he brought back triumphantly.

Sunday, 25 December: Today it is Christmas. What a sad holiday for us all! We have not moved from our casemate (a shellproof enclosure in a fort) for nearly a month. We are filthy; most of our clothes and linen are in chests in town, and we cannot get to them. Mama attempts to clean things as best she can without water. We dare not try to seek any, the danger is too great.... For our holiday meal we turned our tablecloth upside-down and had three bottles of wine and some bread.

31 January: 60th day of bombardment. The town itself has suffered enormously. Most houses are crumbling; there is utter misery. Poor women openly go out into the streets despite the shelling to collect splinters of wood from the remains of their homes.

2 February: This is the worst night we have had since the shelling began.... A huge shell blew up right next to our casemate, killed two men, and injured many....We could hear their screams of agony. Heavens! What a day, and what a night!

13 February: Finally, at 9 A.M. a cease-fire is announced.

TEXTUAL QUESTIONS FOR ANALYSIS

1. Summarize from your text the reasons for the Franco-Prussian War. Do they appear sufficient to justify what you have just read?
2. The Franco-Prussian War was the first major European war to involve large scale civilian casualties, especially in Paris. As is clear from the diary, the Germans used indiscriminate shelling of civilian residential areas as a normal military tactic. Why? Where have you seen the use of such a tactic in recent history and for what reasons?
3. How did the Franco-Prussian War lay the seeds for a future European war?

Source: Bullit Lowry and Elizabeth Gunter, eds., and trans., *The Red Virgin: Memoirs of Louise Michel* (University of Alabama Press, 1981), pp. 19-21.

CHAPTER 42
ADVANCED INDUSTRIAL SOCIETY

Socialism was one of the great political legacies of nineteenth century Europe, just as liberalism was a legacy of the eighteenth century revolutions in Europe and the Americas. Although there were several types of early socialism, by the 1890's, Marxism, with its great theory of class struggle and the inevitable victory of the proletariat over the bourgeoisie, was the dominant variety. But this early Marxism, with its prediction of inevitable class warfare and revolution, was being challenged by a new revision, Social Democracy. The Social Democrats, as they normally called themselves, were distinguished from orthodox Marxists by their policies and programs, not their ideology. They accepted the class struggle theory of history, but believed that the victory of the proletariat in an advanced industrial society must come about through the ballot and peaceful democratic reform, not violent revolution. They considered orthodox Marxists to be impractical and naive, while the orthodox considered such revisionism to be a betrayal of socialism. But their program proved to have great appeal to the labor movement, and in the 1880's and 1890's Social Democratic political parties sprang up in every major industrialized Western European country, and soon became a political force that could influence policy decisions.

Germany became home to one of the most active and powerful Social Democratic parties in Europe before World War I. Although banned until 1890, the party became legal in that year and within a decade had become a major player in Germany's parliamentary system. In 1891 the party held its first official and legal convention in Erfurt, Germany, and adopted a program of political beliefs and aspirations that became a model for Social Democratic parties in other European countries. The following selection, known informally as THE ERFURT PROGRAM, offers an interesting contrast to the Marx's COMMUNIST MANIFESTO. While the latter deals with history and ideology, the former is concerned with immediate programs and laws that can improve the working and living conditions of the working class.

THE ERFURT PROGRAM, 1891

Programme of the Social Democratic Party of Germany

The struggle of the working class against capitalistic exploitation is of necessity a political struggle. The working class cannot carry on its economic contests, and cannot develop its economic organisation, without political rights. It cannot bring about the transference of the means of production into the possession of the community, without having obtained political power.

To give to this fight of the working class a conscious and unified form, and to show it its necessary goal- that is the task of the Social Democratic Party.

The interests of the working class are the same in all countries with a capitalistic mode of production. With the extension of the world's commerce, and of production for the world-market, the position of the worker in every country grows ever more dependent on the position of the worker in other countries. The liberation of the working class, accordingly, is a work in which the workmen of all civilised countries are equally involved. In recognition of this, the Social Democratic Party of Germany feels and declares itself to be one with the class-conscious workmen of all other countries.

The Social Democratic Party of Germany does not fight, accordingly, for new class-privileges and class-rights, but for the abolition of class-rule and of classes themselves, for equal rights and equal duties of all, without distinction of sex or descent. Starting from these views, it combats, within existing society, not only the exploitation and oppression of wage-earners, but every kind of exploitation and oppression, whether directed against a class, a party, a sex, or a race.

Proceeding from these principles, the Social Democratic Party of Germany demands, to begin

with:
1. Universal, equal, and direct suffrage, with secret ballot, for all elections, of all citizens of the realm over twenty years of age, without distinction of sex.... Biennial legislative periods. Holding of the elections on a legal holiday. Compensation of the elected representatives. Abolition of every limitation of political rights, except in the case of legal incapacity.
2. Direct legislation through the people, by means of the rights of proposal and rejection. Self-determination and self-government of the people in realm, state, province, and parish. Election of magistrates by the people, with responsibility to the people. Annual voting of taxes.
3. Education of all to bear arms. Militia in the place of the standing army. Decision by the popular representatives on questions of war and peace. Settlement of all international disputes by arbitration.
4. Abolition of all laws which limit or suppress the right of meeting and coalition.
5. Abolition of all laws which place women, whether in public or a private capacity, at a disadvantage as compared with men.
6. Declaration that religion is a private affair. Abolition of all expenditure of public funds upon ecclesiastical and religious objects. Ecclesiastical and religious bodies are to be regarded as private associations, which regulate their affairs entirely independently.
7. Secularisation of schools. Compulsory attendance at the public national schools. Free education, free supply of educational materials, and free maintenance in the public schools, as well as in the higher educational institutions, for those boys and girls, who, on account of their capacities, are considered fit for further education.
8. Free administration of justice, and free legal assistance. Administration of the law through judges elected by the people. Appeal in criminal cases. Compensation of persons unjustly accused, imprisoned, or condemned. Abolition of capital punishment.
9. Free medical attendance, including midwifery, and free supply of medicines. Free burial.
10. Graduated income and property tax for defraying all public expenses, so far as these are to be covered by taxation. Duty of self-assessment. Inheritance taxes, graduated according to the amount of the inheritance and the degree of relationship. Abolition of all indirect taxes, customs, and other economic measures, which sacrifice the interests of the community to those of a privileged minority....

TEXTUAL QUESTIONS FOR ANALYSIS

1. How is the above program different from the excerpt of the COMMUNIST MANIFESTO that you have in your text?
2. Why would social democracy be feared by capitalists and why would it be welcomed by many working men and women? Relative to women, what are the most revolutionary aspects of this 1891 program?
3. How would points 6, 7, 8, 9, and 10 be of benefit to the working class? What abuses or problems of the working class were they designed to alleviate?
4. Why were points 1, 2, 3, 4, and 5 considered revolutionary in nineteenth century Europe? Who would have been opposed to these points and why?
5. How many of these points have been enacted today in modern Western democracies?

Source: Leslie Derfler, *Socialism Since Marx* (New York: St. Martin's Press, 1973), pp. 36-38.

CHAPTER 43
MODERN SCIENCE AND ITS IMPLICATIONS

In the late nineteenth century Charles Darwin and his theory of evolution, supported by the work of other scientists, changed the view of the educated public toward the history and future of the human race. Although specific aspects of his theory are still debated, the main outlines were accepted by the beginning of the twentieth century. Darwin's work showed that humans were not separate from the natural world, but an integral part of the larger scheme and subject to the same processes as all other living creatures. In addition, humans were shown to have followed the same process of development from simple to more complex forms as other living creatures over the long history of the earth. These were revolutionary ideas in the mid-nineteenth century when Darwin first published his most famous work, THE ORIGIN OF SPECIES, but by the end of the century were widely accepted and formed part of the scientific curriculum of most colleges in Europe and the United States.

Alfred Russel Wallace (1823-1913) was one of the great naturalists of the nineteenth century, and a popularizer and interpreter of Darwin's theory. A Scottish naturalist and a founder of zoological geography, Wallace independently developed his own theory of evolution through the study of animal populations, and became an early and enthusiastic Darwinist. In 1889, seven years after the death of Darwin, Wallace published a work entitled DARWINISM in which he attempted to explain, not only Darwin's major theories and methods, but the impact of the theory thirty years after its publication. The following selection from this book attempts to assess the scope of the changes upon the educated public. It provides an interesting view of just how great a shift in opinion had occurred in only three decades from an involved and dedicated participant.

DARWINISM

The Change of Opinion Effected by Darwin

The point I wish especially to urge is this. Before Darwin's work appeared, the great majority of naturalists, and almost without exception the whole literary and scientific world, held firmly to the belief that species were realities, and had not been derived from other species by any process accessible to us; the different species of crow and of violet were believed to have been always as distinct and separate as they are now, and to have originated by some totally unknown process so far removed from ordinary reproduction that it was usually spoken of as "special creation." There was, then, no question of the origin of families, orders, and classes, because the very first step of all, the "origin of species," was believed to be an insoluble problem. But now this is all changed. The whole scientific and literary world, even the whole educated public, accepts, as a matter of common knowledge, the origin of species from other allied species by the ordinary process of natural birth. The idea of special creation or any altogether exceptional mode of production is absolutely extinct! Yet more: this is held also to apply to many higher groups as well as to the species of a genus, and not even Mr. Darwin's severest critics venture to suggest that the primeval bird, reptile, or fish must have been "specially created." And this vast, this totally unprecedented change in public opinion has been the result of the work of one man, and was brought about in the short space of twenty years! This is the answer to those who continue to maintain that the "origin of species" is not yet discovered; that there are still doubts and difficulties; that there are divergences of structure so great that we cannot understand how they had their beginning. We may admit all this, just as we may admit that there are enormous difficulties in the way of a complete comprehension of the origin and nature of all parts of the solar system and of the stellar universe. But we claim for Darwin that he is the Newton of natural history, and that, just so surely as that the discovery and demonstration by Newton of the law of gravitation established order in place of chaos and laid a sure foundation for all future study of the starry heavens, so surely has Darwin, by his discovery of the law of natural selection and his demonstration of the great principle of the preservation of useful variations in the struggle for life, not only thrown a flood of light on the whole organic world, but also established a firm foundation for all future study of nature.

In order to show the view Darwin took of his own work, and what it was that he alone claimed to have done, the concluding passage of the introduction to THE ORIGIN OF SPECIES should be carefully considered. It is as follows: "Although much remains obscure, and will long remain obscure, I can entertain no doubt, after the most deliberate and dispassionate judgment of which I am capable, that the view which most naturalists until recently entertained and which I formerly entertained- namely, that each species has been independently created- is erroneous. I am fully convinced that species are not immutable; but that those belonging to what are called the same genera are lineal descendants of some other and generally extinct species, in the same manner as the acknowledged varieties of any one species are the descendants of that species. Furthermore, I am convinced that Natural Selection has been the most important, but not the exclusive, means of modification."

It should be especially noted that all which is here claimed is now almost universally admitted, while the criticism of Darwin's works refer almost exclusively to those numerous questions which, as he himself says, "will long remain obscure."

TEXTUAL QUESTIONS FOR ANALYSIS

1. Judging from the above selection, why did some religious leaders question Darwin's conclusions?
2. Summarize what Wallace contends are the most important and accepted portions of Darwin's work? What portions "remain obscure?"
3. How has the work of Darwin changed the study of humanity? What have been the positive benefits of the theory of evolution and natural selection? Have there been any negative aspects?
4. How does the acceptance of Darwin's theories fit in with the general theme of the text chapter concerning the growing importance of science by the beginning of the twentieth century?

Source: Alfred Russell Wallace, *Darwinism* (London: John Murray, 1889), pp. 10-13.

CHAPTER 44
WORLD WAR I AND ITS DISPUTED SETTLEMENT

World War I marks a watershed in the history of the twentieth century. The primacy of Europe was never again as great as it had been in 1914, and it marked the emergence of the United States to the status of a world power. Indeed, it was the intervention of the United States that made an Allied victory possible. The war also spawned a series of revolutions, of which the Communist revolution in Russia would have the greatest consequences. The great tragedy of the war was that it did not settle major issues, and another generation would have to fight again in twenty years.

President Woodrow Wilson (1856-1924) led the United States into the war on a platform that would later be criticized for its naive idealism. Wilson was a reluctant warrior, having won re-election in 1916 in a campaign that emphasized the fact that he had kept America out of the war. But by the spring of 1917, pressured by a resumption of German submarine warfare, concerned about the economic consequences of a Central Powers victory, and convinced that the United States had to play a role in the war if it wanted to play a role in the peace settlement, Wilson asked Congress to declare war on Germany. In his speech to Congress asking for war, Wilson justified America's entry into the war as a great moral crusade which would make the world "safe for democracy," and that the present conflict would become "a war to end all wars." He really did believe that the United States had a special role to play in international affairs due to its disinterested role as a combatant. Alone among the great powers, it had not been directly attacked, did not have any territory occupied by an enemy, and did not seek any territorial concessions. In January, 1918, Wilson announced his plan for the peace settlement after the war, the Fourteen Points. These points summarized for Wilson the reasons for which the war was being fought, and would, he believed, form the basis of a lasting peace settlement. His call for a League of Nations, point fourteen, was for Wilson the most important aspect of his plan, for the League would serve to guarantee the postwar settlement, and eliminate any need for future wars. At the Paris peace conference, Wilson struggled to preserve his plan in the face of British and French opposition. Although the League was one of the few of the Fourteen Points to be actually included in the Versailles Treaty, the U.S. Senate refused to ratify the treaty, and America never joined the League of Nations.

THE FOURTEEN POINTS

We have entered this war because violations of right had occurred which touched us to the quick and made the life of our own people impossible, unless they were corrected, and the world secured once for all against their recurrence.

What we demand in this war, therefore, is nothing peculiar to ourselves. It is that the world be made fit and safe to live in, and particularly that it be made safe for every peace-loving nation which, like our own, wishes to live its own free life, determine its own institutions, be assured of justice and fair dealing by the other peoples of the world, as against force and selfish aggression. All the peoples of the world are in effect partners in this interest, and for our own part we see very clearly that unless justice be done to others it will not be done to us.

The program of the world's peace, therefore, is our program; and that program, the only possible one as we see it, is this:

I. Open covenants of peace, openly arrived at, after which there shall be no private international understandings of any kind, but diplomacy shall proceed always frankly and in the public view.

II. Absolute freedom of navigation upon the seas, outside territorial waters, alike in peace and in war, except as the seas may be closed in whole or in part by international action for the enforcement of international covenants.

III. The removal, so far as possible, of all economic barriers and the establishment of an equality of trade conditions among all the nations consenting to the peace and associating themselves for its maintenance.

IV. Adequate guarantees given and taken that national armaments will be reduced to the lowest point consistent with domestic safety.

V. A free, open-minded, and absolutely impartial adjustment of all colonial claims, based upon a strict observance of the principle that in determining all such questions of sovereignty the interests of the populations concerned must have equal weight with the equitable claims of the Government whose title is to be determined.

VI. The evacuation of all Russian territory, and such a settlement of all questions affecting Russia as will secure the best and freest cooperation of the other nations of the world in obtaining for her an unhampered and unembarrassed opportunity for the independent determination of her own political development and national policy, and assure her of a sincere welcome into the society of free nations under institutions of her own choosing; and , more than a welcome, assistance also of every kind that she may need and may herself desire....

VII. Belgium, the whole world will agree, must be evacuated and restored without any attempt to limit the sovereignty which she enjoys in common with all other free nations....

VIII. All French territory should be freed and the invaded portions restored; and the wrong done to France by Prussia in 1871 in the matter of Alsace-Lorraine, which has unsettled the peace of the world for nearly fifty years, should be righted, in order that peace may once more be made secure in the interest of all.

IX. A readjustment of the frontiers of Italy should be effected along clearly recognizable lines of nationality.

X. The peoples of Austria-Hungary, whose place among the nations we wish to see safe-guarded and assured, should be accorded the freest opportunity of autonomous development.

XI. Rumania, Serbia, and Montenegro should be evacuated; occupied territories restored; Serbia accorded free and secure access to the sea; and the relations of the several Balkan states to one another determined by friendly counsel along historically established lines of allegiance and nationality....

XII. The Turkish portions of the Ottoman Empire should be assured a secure sovereignty, but the other nationalities which are now under Turkish rule should be assured an undoubted security of life and an absolutely unmolested opportunity of autonomous development....

XIII. An independent Polish state should be erected which should include the territories inhabited by indisputably Polish populations, which should be assured a free and secure access to the sea, and whose political and economic independence and territorial integrity should be guaranteed by international covenant.

XIV. A general association of nations must be formed, under specific covenants, for the purpose of affording mutual guaranties of political independence and territorial integrity to great and small nations alike.

In regard to these essential rectifications of wrong and assertions of right we feel ourselves to be the intimate partners of all the Governments and peoples associated together against the imperialists. We cannot be separated in interest or divided in purpose. We stand together until the end.

TEXTUAL QUESTIONS FOR ANALYSIS

1. What are the general and what are the specific parts of the Fourteen Points? Which of the above actually became part of the peace settlement at Versailles?
2. Wilson believed that self-determination of national identify would solve many of Europe's problems. Which of the above points looks to self-determination as a solution? Has nationalism been a solution or a problem for world peace since 1918?
3. Wilson was considered naive in foreign policy by his political opponents. What parts of the Fourteen Points could be used to support their argument that his plan for world peace was not realistic?
4. To consider the realism of his plan, describe what you think might have happened if the Fourteen Points had become the basis of the Treaty of Versailles and the United States had accepted the treaty and joined the League of Nations.

Source: *Congressional Record*, 65th Congress, 2nd session (January 8, 1918), p. 691.

CHAPTER 45
A FRAGILE BALANCE: EUROPE, 1919-1929

The decade after World War I was a period of great change and upheaval in Europe; nowhere were these changes more profound than in Italy. A liberal constitutional monarchy that had achieved national unity only in 1861, Italy had been the most underdeveloped of the major European states at the beginning of the world war. Her government had stayed out of the war, in spite of being a member of the Triple Alliance, for the first year, and had then joined with the Allies because of a promise of territory on the Adriatic coast after the defeat of Austria-Hungary. In spite of huge losses, military defeats in the first two years of the war, and final military success, Prime Minister Orlando returned home from the Versailles conference in anger and humiliation and without any additional territory, defeated by

Wilson's insistence on national self-determination in the Balkans. The war had also shattered Italy's fragile economy; inflation and unemployment created massive labor unrest and led to the rise of a substantial Communist party.

It was in this period of social, political, and economic unrest that Mussolini created his Fascist party. Recruited at first mainly from the ranks of discharged, and often unemployed, veterans, the party denounced the ineffective and weak civilian government, and fought street battles against the Communists. Calling for a national spiritual renewal, Mussolini appealed to more than just the economic woes of the downtrodden. He projected himself and his party as the agents of a new nation-state, a revived Italy that would re-create the glories of the Roman Empire. Mussolini emphasized the emotional and patriotic aspects of his new movement, and predicted that Fascism would create such a sense of spiritual unity among Italians that no nation would be able to stop their drive for greatness. The following selection is an excellent example of Mussolini's early rhetoric and shows the non-rational basis of his appeal. He made this speech on October 24, 1922, only three days before the March on Rome, to the Fascist Congress held in Naples. Its main interest for the student is his clear outline of the Fascist concept of the nation as a spiritual entity that can give purpose and direction to the lives of those who dedicate themselves to it.

MUSSOLINI'S NAPLES SPEECH, OCTOBER 24, 1922

We Fascists have no intention of coming to power by the tradesman's entrance; we Fascists do not intend to turn our backs on the first recruits of our movement, such fearsome and ideal followers, for a miserable dish of ministerial pottage!(Prolonged applause) Because we have a vision of the problem which could be called historical, in contrast to that other vision which could be called political and parliamentary.

It is not a matter of assembling any old government, more dead than alive; it a question of injecting into the liberal State- which has fulfilled tasks which were magnificent and which we will not forget- all the force of the new Italian generations which resulted from the war and our victory.

This is essential not just in the interests of the State, but in the interests of the nation's history.

Well, gentlemen, once the problem is not understood in historical terms, it is transformed into a problem of force. Besides, every time in history deep clashes of interest and ideas surface, it is force which finally decides the issue. This is why we have gathered and tightly organized the ranks of our legions and established an iron discipline in them: to make sure that if the conflict should ever be decided by force, victory will be ours. We deserve it (applause). It is for the Italian people which has the right, which has the duty, to rid its political and spiritual life of all the parasitic encrustations of the past which cannot carry on existing indefinitely in the present because this would kill the future....

We have created our myth. The myth is a faith, a passion. It is not necessary for it to be a reality. It is a reality in the sense that it is a stimulus, is hope, is faith, is courage. Our myth is the nation, our myth is the greatness of the nation! And to this myth, this greatness, which we want to translate into a total reality, we subordinate everything else.

For us the nation is not just territory, but something spiritual. There are States which have had immense territories and which have left no trace in human history. It is not just a question of size, because there have been minute, microscopic States in history which have bequeathed memorable, immortal specimens of art and philosophy.

The greatness of the nation is the totality of all these qualities, of all these conditions. A nation is great when it translates into reality the force of its spirit. Rome became great when, starting out as a small rural democracy, it gradually spread out across the whole of Italy in accordance with its spirit, till it encountered the warriors of Carthage and fought them. It is the first war in history, one of the first. Then, gradually, it bore its standards to the ends of the earth, but at every turn the Roman Empire was the creation of the spirit, since the weapons were aimed, not just by the arms of the Roman legionaries, but by their spirit. Now, therefore, we desire the greatness of the nation, both material and spiritual....

TEXTUAL QUESTIONS FOR ANALYSIS

1. Put into your own words what you think Mussolini meant when he said, "Our myth is the nation, our myth is the greatness of the nation!"
2. Identify the anti-rational and unhistorical elements in this speech. Why was this speech accepted so well in Naples in 1922?
3. Where does the individual and his rights fit into this "myth?" What is to be the role of the individual in this new nation?
4. Are there similar political movements in the world today? Where and how are they similar to Mussolini's message?

Source: Roger Griffin, ed., *Fascism* (New York: Oxford University Press, 1995), pp. 43-44.

CHAPTER 46
THE SOVIET EXPERIMENT TO WORLD WAR II

Lenin led the revolution and won the civil war that created the first communist state in history, but it was his successor Joseph Stalin that created the totalitarian system that would become the hallmark of the Soviet Union until its downfall in 1991. The essential change that Stalin introduced into the system he inherited from Lenin was the creation of a centrally planned economic system in which Communist party leaders assumed the role of planning, mobilizing, and directing all facets of the economy. This system of Five Year Plans, introduced in 1928, established goals for every area of the economy, but was centered on the development of heavy industry and the collectivization of agriculture. Relative to the Western nations, the USSR was economically backward, and Stalin apparently believed that without rapid industrialization the Soviet system would be vulnerable to Western influence and control. He also clearly understood that a system such as he implemented would vastly increase his own power. The human and material cost was staggering, as your text details, but Stalin persisted, and by 1932 was claiming success for his system and proposing goals for the next Five Year Plan.

The following selection is from a speech delivered by Stalin to the Central Committee of the Communist Party in January 1933. His audience consisted of several hundred top ranking Communist party leaders from throughout the Soviet Union, all of whom owed their jobs, titles, power, and prestige to Stalin. These men had been charged by Stalin with carrying out the harsh and brutal schemes of the first Five Year Plan, so Stalin did not try to deceive them for they knew the truth. But his speech was intended for public distribution, so Stalin did try to emphasize the positive and to justify the sacrifices that were required to continue his policies.

THE FIRST FIVE YEAR PLAN, 1933

What was the fundamental task of the five-year plan?

The fundamental task of the five-year plan was to transfer our country, with its backward, and in part medieval, technology, on to the lines of new, modern technology.

The fundamental task of the five-year plan was to convert the U.S.S.R. from an agrarian and weak country, dependent upon the caprices of the capitalist countries, into an industrial and powerful country, fully self-reliant and independent of the caprices of world capitalism.

The fundamental task of the five-year plan was, in converting the U.S.S.R. into an industrial country, to completely oust the capitalist elements, to widen the front of socialist forms of economy, and to create the economic basis for the abolition of classes in the U.S.S.R., for the building of a socialist society....

The fundamental task of the five-year plan was to transfer small and scattered agriculture on to the lines of large-scale collective farming, so as to ensure the economic basis of socialism in the countryside and thus to eliminate the possibility of the restoration of capitalism in the U.S.S.R.

Finally, the task of the five-year plan was to create all the necessary technical and economic prerequisites for increasing to the utmost the defence capacity of the country, enabling it to organise determined resistance to any attempt at military intervention from abroad, to any attempt at military attack from abroad....

The main link in the five-year plan was heavy industry, with machine building as its core. For only heavy industry is capable of reconstructing both industry as a whole, transport and agriculture, and of putting them on their feet. It was necessary to begin the fulfillment of the five-year plan with heavy industry. Consequently, the restoration of heavy industry had to be made the basis of the fulfillment of the five-year plan....

But the restoration and development of heavy industry, particularly in such a backward and poor country as ours was at the beginning of the five-year plan period, is an extremely difficult task; for, as is well known, heavy industry calls for enormous financial expenditure and the existence of a certain minimum of experienced technical forces.... Did the Party know this, and did it take this into account? Yes, it did. Not only did the Party know this, but it announced it for all to hear. The Party knew how heavy industry had been built in Britain, Germany, and America. It knew that in those countries heavy industry had been built either with the aid of big loans, plundering other countries, or by both methods simultaneously. The Party knew that those paths were closed to our country. What, then, did it count on? It counted on our country's own resources. It counted on the fact that, with a Soviet government at the helm, and the land, industry, transport, the banks and trade nationalised, we could pursue a regime of the strictest economy in order to accumulate sufficient resources for the restoration and development of heavy industry. The Party declared frankly that this would call for serious sacrifices, and that it was our duty openly and consciously to make these sacrifices if we wanted to achieve our goal....

What are the results of the five-year plan in four years in the sphere of industry?

We did not have an iron and steel industry, the basis for the industrialisation of the country.

Now we have one.
    We did not have a tractor industry. Now we have one.
    We did not have an automobile industry. Now we have one.
    We did not have a machine-tool industry. Now we have one.
    We did not have a big and modern chemical industry. Now we have one.
    We did not have a real and big industry for the production of modern agricultural machinery. Now we have one.
    We did not have an aircraft industry. Now we have one.
    In output of electrical power we were last on the list. Now we rank among the first.
    In output of oil products and coal we were last on the list. Now we rank among the first....

Finally, as a result of all this the Soviet Union has been converted from a weak country, unprepared for defence, into a country mighty in defence, a country prepared for every contingency, a country capable of producing on a mass scale all modern means of defence and of equipping its army with them in the event of an attack from abroad....

TEXTUAL QUESTIONS FOR ANALYSIS

1. Summarize what Stalin said were the objectives of the five-year plan? Who or what is going to be in charge of implementing these changes according to Stalin?
2. How is this speech different from what a prime minister or president of a western democracy might have said in reviewing the achievements of a parliamentary government?
3. What does Stalin say are the results of the first five-year plan? Why do you think he does not give specific figures in his speech?
4. What were the human costs of his five-year plan that he omitted from his speech? Did he make any factual errors in his account of how Western countries had industrialized?

Source: Joseph Stalin, "The Tasks of Business Executives" (speech at the First Union Conference of Managers of Soviet Industry, January 1933) in *Problems of Leninism*

(Moscow: 1940), pp. 359-360, 365-366.

CHAPTER 47
TOTALITARIANISM: THE NAZI STATE

Adolf Hitler was the supreme leader of one of the most destructive and powerful states of the modern world, the Nazi regime of Germany from 1933 to 1945. But the world should not have been surprised by his policies, for he outlined them at length and publicly for years before coming to power as Chancellor of Germany in January 1933. World War I had been the pivotal event in his life. Serving for four years on the Western front, he had been a capable and dedicated soldier, receiving medals for bravery under fire. Believing Germany betrayed by Jews and Communists after the war, he joined and soon led the small Munich-based National Socialist German Workers Party (abbreviated as NAZI). In 1920 this party adopted a platform that was radically nationalist and racist. It called for the unification of all Germans in Europe into one state, the removal of Jewish influence in German life, the creation of living space for Germans by the conquest of territory in eastern Europe, and an end to the restrictions and reparations placed upon Germany by the Versailles treaty. Hitler greatly admired his contemporary Mussolini, and in 1923 attempted to emulate the latter's successful March on Rome by leading an attempt to overthrow the state government of Bavaria through an armed march on the city hall in Munich. But Munich was not Rome, and the authorities crushed the Nazi march with armed force, arrested Hitler, and put him on trial for treason. Due to his war record and wide spread sympathy for his nationalistic views, he received a short five-year sentence, and served only eight and a half months in relative comfort.

Hitler became convinced by the failure of the Munich march that the Nazi party would have to win political power through the ballot, and that the party needed to organize itself for a long political struggle. To this end he used his time in prison to dictate his memoirs. These were intended to encourage the faithful and instruct the undecided. The final manuscript ran to some eight hundred pages, and was entitled MEIN KAMPF (My Struggle). It was part autobiography, part political history, and part political philosophy. In this long rambling work, Hitler presented his nationalistic and racist theories about world and European history, and clearly indicated what he would do if he ever came to power. The book became a best seller after Hitler came to power in 1933, and by 1943 there were almost ten million copies in print. It became a favorite marriage and birthday gift, and even made Hitler a wealthy man. The following selection presents Hitler's conception of Aryan supremacy and the basis for his anti-Semitism.

MEIN KAMPF

If one were to divide mankind into three groups: culture-founders, culture-bearers, and culture destroyers, then, as representative of the first kind, only the Aryan would come in question. It is from him that the foundation and the walls of all human creations originate, and only the external form and color depend on the characteristics of the various peoples involved. He furnishes the gigantic building-stones and also the plans for all human progress, and only the execution corresponds to the character of the people and races in the various instances....

The progress of mankind resembles the ascent of an endless ladder; one cannot arrive at the top without first having taken the lower steps. Thus the Aryan had to go the way which reality showed him and not that of which the imaginations of a modern pacifist dreams. The way of reality, however, is hard and difficult, but it finally ends where the other wishes to bring mankind by dreaming, but unfortunately removes it from, rather than brings it nearer to, it.

Therefore, it is no accident that the first cultures originated in those places where the Aryan, by meeting lower peoples, subdued them and made them subject to his will. They, then, were the first technical instrument in the service of a growing culture.

With this the way that the Aryan had to go was clearly lined out. As a conqueror he subjected the lower peoples and then he regulated their practical ability according to his command and his will and for his aims.... As long as he kept up ruthlessly the master's standpoint, he not only really remained "master" but also the preserver and propagator of the culture.... But as soon as the subjected peoples themselves began to rise and approached the conqueror linguistically, the sharp separating wall between master and slave fell. The Aryan gave up the purity of his blood and therefore he also lost his place in the Paradise which he had created for himself.... For some time he may still live on the existing cultural goods, but then petrifaction sets in, and finally oblivion....

The blood-mixing, however, with the lowering of the racial level caused by it, is the sole cause of the dying-off of old cultures; for the people do not perish by lost wars, but by the loss of that force of resistance which is contained only in the pure blood.

All that is not race in this world is trash.

All world historical events, however, are the expression of the races' instinct of self-preservation in its good or in its evil meaning....

The Jew forms the strongest contrast to the Aryan. Hardly in any people of the world is the instinct of self-preservation more strongly developed that in the so-called "chosen people." The fact of the existence of this race alone may be looked upon as the best proof of this. Where is the people that in the past two thousand years has been exposed to so small changes of the inner disposition, of character, etc., as the Jewish people? Which people finally has experienced greater changes than this one- and yet has always come forth the same form the most colossal catastrophes of mankind? What an infinitely persistent will for life, for preserving the race do these facts disclose!....

No, the Jew possesses no culture-creating energy whatsoever, as the idealism, without which there can never exist a genuine development of man towards a higher level, does not and never did exist in him. His intellect, therefore, will never have a constructive effect, but only a destructive one.

A racially pure people, conscious of its blood, can never be enslaved by the Jew. It will forever only be the master of bastards in this world.

Thus he systematically tries to lower the racial level by a permanent poisoning of the individual.

In the political sphere, however, he begins to replace the idea of democracy by that of the dictatorship of the proletariat.

In the organized mass of Marxism he has found the weapon which makes him now dispense with democracy and which allows him, instead, to enslave and to "rule" the people dictatorially with the brutal fist.

He now works methodically towards the revolution in a twofold direction: economically and politically....

In the domain of culture he infects art, literature, theater, smites natural feeling, overthrows all conceptions of beauty and sublimity, of nobility and quality, and in turn he pulls the people down into the confines of his own swinish nature....

If we let all the causes of the German collapse pass before our eyes, there remains as the ultimate and decisive cause the non-recognition of the race problem and especially of the Jewish danger....

TEXTUAL QUESTIONS FOR ANALYSIS

1. According to Hitler what is the historical role of the Aryan race? What is the danger to the Aryans?
2. According to Hitler, what is the danger posed by the Jewish race? What twentieth century political philosophy does he identify as the mechanism used by the Jewish race to bring about political revolution?
3. What was the source of Germany's defeat in World War I according to Hitler? What is the logical consequence of accepting his ideas?
4. Why might these ideas have had some appeal to the Germans of the 1920's and 1930's? Can you cite instances where these ideas are still to be found?

Source: Adolph Hitler, *Mein Kampf* (Boston: Houghton Mifflin, 1971), pp. 398-399, 418, 451-455.

CHAPTER 48
EAST ASIA IN A CENTURY OF CHANGE, 1840-1940

No Asian country went through a greater and more fundamental series of changes than Japan in the period 1840-1940. From its feudal isolation under the Tokugawa Shogunate in the mid-nineteenth century, Japan had become by 1940 a modern industrialized state intent on creating a vast Asian empire for itself by military expansion in imitation of Western imperialism. These changes brought with them great tension and turbulence as Japan sought to modernize its economy, government, and society. In the 1920's and 1930's various patriotic organizations emerged in Japan, often affiliated with associations of young military officers, that called for extreme nationalism and an end to the civilian government that they viewed as corrupt and uninterested in the plight of the common people. These young army officers were especially critical of what they viewed as the government's favoritism toward big business, the policies of accommodation with the Western powers, and the reluctance of the civilian government to embark on a policy of expansionism toward China. What they admired were the fascist and socialist policies of Italy and Russia, and what they sought was a government that would combine what they considered to be the best aspects of both systems. In 1931 it was a group of young army officers that provoked Japanese intervention into Manchuria, and in 1932 Premier Inukai Tsuyoshi was assassinated by a group of officers seeking to end Japan's parliamentary system of government and restore all political power to the emperor. On February 26, 1936, over a thousand troops and officers of the army's elite First Division seized the center of Tokyo, assassinated several Cabinet officials, and called upon the emperor to join them. The insurrection was crushed, and most of the ringleaders were executed, but the influence of the army over the government greatly increased over the following months, and within a year Japan's military leaders had pushed the country into a full-scale invasion of China, an action which would eventually lead to her to war with the United States.

One of the leading critics of big business and the parliamentary system was Kita Ikki (1883-1937). He was a radical nationalist who believed in Japan's imperial mission of ousting the Western powers from Asia, establishing an economic empire based on land in China, and a government centered on the emperor at home. He also called for an end to favoritism for big business and a government that would provide benefits to the working classes. His most influential book was AN OUTLINE FOR THE RECONSTRUCTION OF JAPAN, written in exile in 1919 in Shanghai. He favored immediate and drastic changes, calling for revolution by the military if necessary, to carry out these policies. His ideas and works became very popular with many young officers, and he was identified as the intellectual founder of the various patriotic organizations that sprang up in the 1920's and 1930's. Although he did not participate in the 1936 revolt in Tokyo, his ideas were considered the prime inspiration of the young officers who led that bloody action, so he was arrested and executed for treason by the government, becoming a martyr to the cause of extreme nationalism.

AN OUTLINE FOR THE RECONSTRUCTION OF JAPAN

Section 1. The Emperor of the People

Suspension of the Constitution: In order to establish a firm base for national reorganization, the Emperor, with the aid of the entire Japanese nation and by invoking his imperial prerogatives, shall suspend the constitution for a period of three years, dissolve the two houses of the Diet, and place the entire country under martial law.

The true significance of the Emperor: We must make clear the fundamental principle that the

Emperor is the sole representative of the people and the pillar of the state.

To clarify this doctrine, there shall be a instituted a sweeping reform in the imperial court, consistent with the spirit shown by Emperor Jimmu in the founding of the nation and by Emperor Meiji in the Restoration. The incumbent Privy Councillors and other officials shall be replaced by men of ability, sought throughout the realm, capable of assisting the Emperor.

An Advisory Council shall be established to assist the Emperor. Its members, fifty in number, shall be appointed by the Emperor.

Whenever the Cabinet Council so decides or the Diet places a vote of non-confidence against him, an Advisory Council member shall submit his resignation to the Emperor. However, this procedure shall not be interpreted to mean that Council members are responsible to the Cabinet or the Diet.

Abolition of the peerage system: By abolishing the peerage system, we shall be able to remove the feudal aristocracy which constitutes a barrier between the Emperor and the people. In this way the spirit of the Meiji Restoration shall be proclaimed.

The House of Peers shall be replaced by the Deliberative Council which shall review decisions made by the House of Representatives. The Deliberative Council may reject for a single time only any decisions of the House of Representatives.

The members of the Deliberative Council shall consist of men distinguished in various fields of activities, elected by each other or appointed by the Emperor.

Popular election: All men twenty-five years of age and above shall have the right to elect and be elected to the House of Representatives, exercising their rights with full equality as citizens of Great Japan. Similar provisions shall apply to all local self-governing bodies. No women shall be permitted to participate in politics....

Section 2: Limitation on Private Property

Limitation on private property: No Japanese family shall possess property in excess of one million yen. A similar limitation shall apply to Japanese citizens holding property overseas. No one shall be permitted to make a gift of property to those related by blood or to others, or to transfer his property by other means with the intent of circumventing this limitation.

Nationalization of excess amount over limitation on private property: Any amount which exceeds the limitation on private property shall revert to the state without compensation....

Section 5: Rights of Workers

Functions of the Ministry of Labor: A Ministry of Labor shall be established within the Cabinet to protect the rights of all workers employed by state-owned and privately-owned industries. Industrial disputes shall be submitted to the Ministry of Labor for arbitration.... This arbitration shall be uniformly binding on all industrial ministries, private industries, and workers....

Working hours: Working hours shall be uniformly set at eight hours a day. Wages shall be paid for Sundays and holidays when no work is performed. Farm workers shall receive additional wages for the overtime work performed during the busy farming seasons.

Distribution of profits to workers: One half of the net profits of private industries shall be distributed to workers employed in such industries....

Workers employed in state-owned industries shall received semi-annual bonuses in lieu of the profit distribution....

Women's labor: Women's labor shall be free and equal to that of men. However, after the reorganization, the state shall make it a matter of national policy that the burden of labor shall not rest on the shoulders of women. In order to prepare women to replace men in providing needed labor in a national emergency, women shall receive education equal to that of men....

Section 8: Rights of the State

Continuation of the conscript system: The state, having rights to existence and development among the nations of the world, shall maintain the present conscript system in perpetuity.... Soldiers in active service shall receive stipends from the state. In the army bases and warships, there shall be no difference in the enjoyment of provisions among the officers, soldiers, and seamen except the emblems signifying their respective ranks....

TEXTUAL QUESTIONS FOR ANALYSIS

1. What are the fascist and what are the socialist aspects of the above plan?
2. What is Ikki's view of the role of the emperor? Are there any similarities between his views and those of the reading in Chapter 41 on the virtues of the samurai?
3. What are the contradictions in his proposals regarding women? Account for these contradictions.
4. Why do you think young army officers were attracted to the writings of Ikki?

Source: David John Lu, ed., *Sources of Japanese History* (Boston: McGraw-Hill, 1974), Vol. 2, pp. 131-136

CHAPTER 49
WORLD WAR II

The anti-Semitic policies and theories of Aryan supremacy of Adolf Hitler reached their nightmarish conclusion in the death camps created by the Nazis after the invasion of Russia in 1941. The Holocaust would eventually claim an estimated six million Jewish victims and about three million non-Jews. One of the reasons that so much detail is known about this policy of genocide is that the Nazis kept detailed records and at the end of the war this evidence was used against leading Nazis at the Nuremburg War Crimes Trials. One of the most infamous camps was Auschwitz in southern Poland, in which an estimated two to three million victims were murdered or died of disease, overwork, or mistreatment. In 1946 at the Nuremburg Tribunal, Rudolf Hoess, the former commandant of Auschwitz was tried for crimes against humanity, found guilty, and sentenced to death. The following selection is a portion of his own testimony in which he gives a candid and detailed explanation of the policy of extermination. He expressed no regret throughout his trial, contending that he was only a loyal Nazi official carrying out a difficult assignment. He expressed pride in the technical refinements he introduced into his factory of death, and seemed bewildered that his actions should be considered subject to prosecution, for, as he said, he did not decide on the policy, he simply carried it out.

TESTIMONY OF RUDOLF HOESS, NUREMBURG, 1946

....I have been constantly associated with the administration of concentration camps since 1934, serving at Dachau until 1938; then as Adjutant in Sachsenhausen from 1938 to 1 May 1940, when I was appointed Commandant of Auschwitz. I commanded Auschwitz until 1 December 1943, and estimate that at least 2,500,000 victims were executed and exterminated there by gassing and burning, and at least another half million succumbed to starvation and disease, making a total dead of about 3,000,000. This figure represents about 70 or 80 percent of all persons sent to Auschwitz as prisoners, the remainder having been selected and used for slave labor in the concentration camp industries; included among the executed and burned were approximately 20,000 Russian prisoners of war who were delivered at Auschwitz in Wehrmacht (German army) transports operated by regular Wehrmacht officers and men. The remainder of the total number of victims included about 100,000 German Jews, and great numbers of citizens, mostly Jewish, from Holland, France, Belgium, Poland, Hungary, Czechoslovakia, Greece, or other countries. We executed about 400,000 Hungarian Jews at Auschwitz in the summer of 1944....

The "final solution" of the Jewish question meant the complete extermination of all Jews in Europe. I was ordered to establish extermination facilities at Auschwitz in June 1941. At that time, there were already in the General Government (western Poland) three other extermination camps: Belzek, Treblinka, and Wolzek.... I visited Treblinka to find out how they carried out their exterminations. The camp commandant at Treblinka told me that he had liquidated 80,000 in the course of one-half year. He was principally concerned with liquidating all the Jews from the Warsaw Ghetto. He used monoxide gas (truck engine emissions), and I did not think that his methods were very efficient. So, when I set up the extermination building at Auschwitz, I used Cyklon B, which was a crystallized prussic acid which we dropped into the death chamber from a small opening. It took from 3 to 15 minutes to kill the people in the death chamber, depending upon climatic conditions. We knew when the people were dead because their screaming stopped. We usually waited about one-half hour before we opened the doors and removed the bodies. After the bodies were removed our special Kommandos (Jewish prisoners who were gassed after doing this job for several weeks) took off the rings and extracted the gold from the teeth of the corpses....

Another improvement we made over Treblinka was that we built our gas chamber to accommodate 2,000 people at one time whereas at Treblinka their gas chambers only accommodated 200 people each. The way we selected our victims was as follows: We had two SS doctors on duty at Auschwitz to examine the incoming transports of prisoners. The prisoners would be marched by one of the doctors who would make spot decisions as they walked by. Those who were fit for work were sent into the camp. Others were sent immediately to the extermination plants. Children of tender years were invariably exterminated since by reason of their youth they were unable to work. Still another improvement we made over Treblinka was that at Triblinka the victims almost always knew that they were to be exterminated and at Auschwitz we endeavored to fool the victims into thinking that they were to go through a delousing process. Of course, frequently they realized our true intentions and we sometimes had riots and difficulties due to that fact. Very frequently women would hide their children under the clothes, but of course when we found them we would send the children in to be exterminated. We were required to carry out these exterminations in secrecy but of course the foul and nauseating stench from the continuous burning of bodies permeated the entire area and all of the people living in the surrounding communities knew that exterminations were going on at Auschwitz.

TEXTUAL QUESTIONS FOR ANALYSIS

1. What are the improvements that Hoess says he introduced at Auschwitz?
2. What were the criteria used to select those to be killed immediately, and those who would be used for slave labor in the industrial plants of the camp?
3. How was this system of mass murder a logical outgrowth of the ideas presented in Hitler's MEIN KAMPF that you read in Chapter 50?
4. One of the most perplexing questions concerning Nazism and the Holocaust is how could a system so destructive of human life and values arise in a civilized society such as Germany? Based on your text and documents readings, attempt an answer.

Source: *Internatioal Military Tribunal (Nuremburg Trial)* Document 3868-PS, XXXIII, pp. 275-276.

CHAPTER 50
HIGH AND LOW CULTURES IN THE WEST

The devastation and horror caused by two great world conflicts in less than thirty years produced a great crisis of confidence among Western intellectuals. The First World War had caused many writers and artists to question basic Western assumptions, such as the notion of human material and spiritual progress advancing ever upward and the concept of a divine purpose to life, but World War II completed the process of disillusionment for many. In the face of events such as the Holocaust and massive civilian casualties from bombing, it was increasingly difficult to cling to notions of scientific progress and divine purpose. Existentialism developed from this rejection of the optimistic outlook based on a faith in modern science that had characterized Western culture before 1914.

Jean-Paul Sartre (1905-1980) became the leading philosopher of existentialism in the postwar West. Born in Paris, he was too young to serve in the trenches of World War I, but old enough to observe the effects produced by this great calamity. He became a writer in the 1930's and served in the French Resistance during World War II. His major work, EXISTENTIALISM, was published in 1946 and established his reputation as the foremost philosophical writer of his day. He wrote novels and dramas as well as philosophical works, but it was his writings on existentialism that made his reputation. The following selection is from a book he published in 1957, attempting to explain the new philosophy that had become by that time a popular success.

EXISTENTIALISM AND HUMAN EMOTIONS

What is meant by the term *existentialism*? Most who use the word would be rather embarrassed if they had to explain it, since, now that the word is all the rage, even the work of a musician or painter is being called existentialist....

Atheistic existentialism, which I represent,....states that if God does not exist, there is at least one being in whom existence precedes essence, a being who exists before he can be defined by any concept, and that this being is man, or,....human reality. What is meant here by saying that existence precedes essence? It means that, first of all, man exists, turns up, appears on the scene, and only afterwards, defines himself. If man, as the existentialist conceives him, is indefinable, it is because at first he is nothing. Only afterward will he be something, and he himself will have made what he will be. Thus, there is no human nature, since there is no God to conceive it. Not only is man what he conceives himself to be, but he is also only what he wills himself to be after his thrust toward existence.

Man is nothing else but what he makes of himself. Such is the first principle of existentialism.... Thus, existentialism's first move is to make every man aware of what he is and to make the full responsibility of his existence rest on him. And when we say that a man is responsible for himself, we do not only mean that he is responsible for his own individuality, but that he is responsible for all men.
   Thus, our responsibility is much greater than we might have supposed, because it involves all mankind.... This helps us understand what the actual content is of such rather grandiloquent words as anguish, forlornness, despair. As you will see, it's all quite simple.

First, what is meant by anguish? The existentialists say at once that man is anguish. What this means is this: the man who involves himself and who realizes that he is not only the person he chooses to be, but also a lawmaker who is, at the same time, choosing all mankind as well as himself, cannot help escape the feeling of his total and deep responsibility.... All leaders know this anguish. That doesn't keep them from acting; on the contrary, it is the very condition of their action. For it implies that they envisage a number of possibilities, and when they choose one, they realize that it has value only because it is chosen. We shall see that this kind of anguish, which is the kind that existentialism describes, is explained, in addition, by a direct responsibility to the other men whom it involves. It is not a curtain separating us from action, but is part of action itself.

When we speak of forlornness.... we mean only that God does not exist and that we have to face all the consequences of this. The existentialist is strongly opposed to a certain kind of secular ethics which would like to abolish God with the least possible expense.... The existentialist, on the contrary, thinks it very distressing that God does not exist, because all possibility of finding values in a heaven of ideas disappears along with Him; there can no longer be an ideal Good, since there is no infinite and perfect consciousness to think it.... Indeed, everything is permissible, if God does not exist, and as a result man is forlorn, because neither within him nor without does he find anything to cling to. He can't start making excuses for himself....

That is the idea I shall try to convey when I say that man is condemned to be free. Condemned, because he did not create himself, yet, in other respects is free; because, once thrown into the world, he is responsible for everything he does....

The existentialist does not think that man is going to help himself by finding in the world some omen by which to orient himself. Because he thinks that man will interpret the omen to suit himself. Therefore, he thinks that man, with no support and with no aid, is condemned every moment to invent man....

Existentialism is nothing else than an attempt to draw all the consequences of a coherent atheistic position. It isn't trying to plunge man into despair at all. But if one calls every attitude of unbelief despair, like the Christians, then the word is not being used in its original sense. Existentialism isn't so atheistic that it wears itself out showing that God doesn't exist. Rather, it declares that even if God did exist, that would change nothing. There you've got your point of view. Not that we believe that God exists, but we think that the problem of His existence is not the issue. In this sense existentialism is optimistic, a doctrine of action, and it is plain dishonesty for Christians to make no distinction between their own despair and ours and then to call us despairing.

TEXTUAL QUESTIONS FOR ANALYSIS

1. According to Sartre, what must every person do and what is the limit of individual responsibility for one's actions?
2. Sartre was accused of being a philosopher of despair. How does he answer this charge?
3. Give a list of reasons, based on your text and document readings, for the spread of atheism in the period of the 1930's and 1940's.
4. How does Sartre define anguish, forlornness, and despair?

Source: Wade Baskin, ed., *Jean-Paul Satre, The Philosophy of Existentialism* (New York: The Philosophical Library, Inc., 1965), pp. 34-37.

CHAPTER 51
SUPERPOWER RIVALRY AND THE EUROPEAN RECOVERY

The United States found itself in a unique position in 1945 at the end of World War II; it was the richest nation in the world and had suffered no physical damage from the most destructive war in human history. The nations of Western Europe had been shattered, economically and physically, by the war. The Soviet Union, although it had suffered enormous destruction at the hands of the Germans, emerged from the war as the master of Eastern Europe, and the major competitor of the United States in terms of political influence in Europe. By 1947 the United States, under President Truman, looked upon the Soviet Union as a potential enemy, and sought to oppose the growing influence of Communism in Western Europe with the Marshall Plan. The plan was rooted in the conviction that the economic distress of nations such as France and Italy might prove to be a fertile breeding ground for home-grown Communist parties, and that Communist governments might come to power through the ballot box as impoverished Europeans looked for some quick solution to their problems. Economic growth and recovery was seen by President Truman and Secretary of State Marshall as the remedy for this danger. But this policy meant a major departure in American foreign affairs, for the United States would have to supply the funds to begin this process, and would have to maintain a sizeable military and political presence in Europe to safeguard the investment and promote the growth of democratic governments, something it had not been prepared to do after World War I. Truman and Marshall jointly developed the policy, but faced with a hostile Republican Congress, Truman allowed George Marshall, a popular retired general who had been the Chairman of the Joint Chiefs of Staff during the war, to introduce the new policy in the commencement address at Harvard University on June 5, 1947. By November the plan was being debated in Congress and Marshall appeared before a joint House and Senate Committee to defend this new foreign policy. When approved, the plan meant that the United States looked upon a stable, prosperous, and anti-Communist Europe as vital to its national security, and was prepared to spend enormous sums to promote European recovery. The Marshall Plan became a cornerstone of American policy throughout the first decade of the Cold War, and turned out to be a rousing success, as Western Europe experienced rapid economic growth in the 1950's.

SECRETARY OF STATE MARSHALL BEFORE CONGRESS, NOVEMBER 10, 1947

The Congress in the coming session will be called upon to make decisions which, although less spectacular and dramatic, will be no less important for the future of our country and the world than those of the war years....

The President will lay before the Congress the program of his administration for aid to Europe. My duty as Secretary of State is to present the reasons for this program; the reasons why I profoundly believe that the vital interest of the United States is directly involved....

As a result of the war, the European community which for centuries had been one of the most productive and indeed creative portions of the inhabited world was left prostrate. This area, despite its diversity of national cultures and its series of internecine conflicts and wars, nonetheless enjoys a common heritage and a common civilization.

The war ended with the armies of the major Allies meeting in the heart of this community. The policies of three of them have been directed to the restoration of that European community. It is now clear that only one power, the Soviet Union, does not for its own reasons share this aim.

We have become involved in two wars which have had their origins in the European continent. The free peoples of Europe have fought two wars to prevent the forcible domination of their community by a single great power. Such domination would have inevitably menaced the stability and security of the world. To deny today our interest in their ability to defend their own heritage would be to disclaim the efforts and sacrifices of two generations of Americans. We wish to see this community restored as one of the pillars of world security; in a position to renew its contribution to the advancement of mankind and to the development of a world order based on law and respect for the individual....

The present line of division in Europe is roughly the line upon which the Anglo-American armies coming from the west met those of the Soviet Union coming from the east. To the west of that line the nations of the continental European community have been grappling with the vast and difficult problem resulting from the war in conformity with their own national traditions without pressure or menace from the United States or Great Britain. Developments in the European countries to the east of that line bear the unmistakable imprint of an alien hand. All the nations of Europe, 16 in number, which were in a position to exercise free choice gave a prompt and energetic response to the simple suggestion made at Harvard on June 5 and thereby an impressive demonstration of the continuing vitality of European civilization.

It would be well, therefore, to deal briefly with what the area encompassed by those 16 nations plus western Germany has meant to us and has meant to the world. This community before the war accounted for nearly one-half of the world's trade. They owned nearly two-thirds of the world's shipping. Their industrial production in terms of the basic commodities of coal, steel, and chemicals was before the war slightly greater than that of the United States. Their economy was highly integrated, each part depending upon the efficient working of the other.

I think that the figures cited will indicate the importance, even from a purely economic point of view, of the 16 nations who have joined together to develop a program for their mutual recovery. Their response to our suggestion of June 5 was a remarkable cooperative effort in a postwar world in which that element has hitherto been distressingly lacking....

The automatic success of the program cannot be guaranteed. The imponderables are many. The risks are real. They are, however, risks which have been carefully calculated, and I believe the chances of success are good. There is convincing evidence that the peoples of western Europe want to preserve their free society and the heritage we share with them. To make that choice conclusive they need our assistance. It is in the American tradition to help. In helping them we will be helping ourselves- because in the larger sense our national interests coincide with those of a free and prosperous Europe.

We must not fail to meet this inspiring challenge. We must not permit the free community of Europe to be extinguished.... Whether we like it or not, we find ourselves, our Nation, in a world position of vast responsibility. We can act for our own good by acting for the world's good.

TEXTUAL QUESTIONS FOR ANALYSIS

1. According to Secretary of State Marshall, what is the source of the threat to western Europe? What has created the division of Europe and what is the division?
2. How important was Europe economically before the war?
3. To what does Marshall appeal in his call for assistance to Europe: self-interest, morality, or both? Explain.
4. Congress did pass the Marshall Plan, and eventually over $30 billion would be spent to assist Western European economic recovery. What were the long-term consequences economically, politically, and militarily?

Source: *Department of State Bulletin,* November 15, 1947, pp. 1159-1161.

CHAPTER 52
DECOLONIZATION AND THE "THIRD WORLD"

Mohandas K. Gandhi (1869-1948) is rightly regarded as the spiritual and philosophical father of Indian independence. His policy of *satyagraha,* translated loosely as "firmness in truth," was developed in South Africa during his struggles there against racial and economic discrimination against Indians. He further developed this policy of non-violent resistance against oppression when he returned to India during World War I. In the 1920's and 1930's his policy and personality provided enlightened guidance to India's struggle for independence. Even British politicians who disagreed with him and fought to keep India under imperial control were forced to admire his resolution and his high principles. Martin Luther King Jr. would later find guidance from Gandhi's life and principles during the Civil Rights struggle against racial segregation in the southern United States.

Gandhi was a prolific writer; the official collection of his published works runs to sixty-four volumes. He began his writing career in South Africa and continued until shortly before his assassination in 1948. The following selection is from an article he published in 1938 describing his faith in non-violence.

NON-VIOLENCE

I have found that life persists in the midst of destruction and, therefore, there must be a higher law than that of destruction. Only under that law would a well-ordered society be intelligible and life worth living. And if that is the law of life, we have to work it out in daily life. Wherever there are wars, wherever you are confronted with an opponent, conquer him with love. In a crude manner I have it worked out in my life. That does not mean that all my difficulties are solved. I have found, however, that this law of love has answered as the law of destruction has never done. In India we have had an ocular demonstration of the operation of this law on the widest scale possible. I do not claim therefore that non-violence has necessarily penetrated the three hundred millions, but I do claim that it has penetrated deeper than any other message, and in an incredibly short time. We have not been all uniformly non-violent; and with the vast majority, non-violence has been a matter of policy. Even so, I want you to find out if the country has not made phenomenal progress under the protecting power of non-violence.

It takes a fairly strenuous course of training to attain to a mental state of non-violence. In daily life it has to be a course of discipline though one may not like it, like for instance, the life of a soldier. But I agree that, unless there is a hearty co-operation of the mind, the mere outward observance will be simply a mask, harmful both to the man himself and to others. The perfect state is reached only when mind and body and speech are in proper co-ordination. But it is always a case of intense mental struggle. It is not that I am incapable of anger, for instance, but I succeed on almost all occasions to keep my feelings under control. Whatever may be the result, there is always in me a conscious struggle for following the law of non-violence deliberately and ceaselessly. Such a struggle leaves one stronger for it. Non-violence is the weapon of the strong. With the weak it might easily be hypocrisy. Fear and love are contradictory terms. Love is reckless in giving away, oblivious as to what it gets in return. Love wrestles with the world as with the self and ultimately gains a mastery over all other feelings. My daily experience, as of those who are working with me, is that every problem lends itself to solution if we are determined to make the law of truth and non-violence the law of life. For truth and non-violence are, to me, faces of the same coin.

The law of love will work, just as the law of gravitation will work, whether we accept it or not. Just as a scientist will work wonders out of various applications of the laws of nature, even so a man who applies the law of love with scientific precision can work greater wonders. For the force of non-violence is infinitely more wonderful and subtle than the material forces of nature, like, for instance, electricity. The men who discovered for us the law of love were greater scientists than any of our modern scientists. Only our explorations have not gone far enough and so it is not possible for every one to see all its working. Such, at any rate, is the hallucination, if it is one, under which I am laboring. The more I work at this law the more I feel the delight in life, the delight in the scheme of this universe. It gives me a peace and a meaning of the mysteries of nature that I have no power to describe.

TEXTUAL QUESTIONS FOR ANALYSIS

1. Gandhi says the "law of love" will work, but how does he apparently expect it to work? Is Gandhi an optimist or a pessimist in his view of human nature?
2. Why did the British authorities have such a difficult time dealing with ideas and policies such as the selection outlines? Do you think Gandhi would have similar success attempting to change Stalin's policies in Russia in the 1930's?
3. What does he mean when he says that non-violence is "a weapon of the strong?" Is this the usual interpretation of non-violence?
4. What are the Hindu and the Christian elements in his concept of non-violence?

Source: M. K. Gandhi, "Satyagraha," in *Young India, March 23, 1921* (Ahmedabad, India: Navajivan Trust)

CHAPTER 53
THE NEW ASIA

The leadership of Mao Zedong (1893-1976) was central to the success of the Communists in China. Born into a well-to-do peasant family in central China, Mao received a traditional Confucian education in the local elementary school, but his life and education were changed forever by the events that swept China during his adolescent years. In 1911 the revolution against the old Imperial system actually broke out, and Mao served briefly in the army. After a brief and unimpressive tour of duty, he was mustered out in 1912, and attended a western style teachers' college in Chang-sha, the capital of his home province of Hunan. This college exposed him to Western-style subjects, such as foreign history and geography, and encouraged its students to join in the effort to modernize and reform China. After graduation from Chang-sha in 1918, he enrolled in Beijing University to complete his education. His year here was to prove crucial to the rest of his life. He was exposed to and rapidly adopted the new doctrines of Marxism-Leninism, becoming in 1921 one of the founding members of the Chinese Communist Party. During the 1920's he became one of the leaders of the young revolutionary movement, and in the mid-1930's consolidated his position to become the undisputed leader of the party. He successfully led the Communists through the period of cooperation against the Japanese, 1937-1945, and from 1946-1949 mounted an ultimately victorious military campaign against the Kuomintang or Nationalist party of Chiang Kai-Shek. In Beijing in January 1949, with the Nationalists defeated and retreating to Taiwan, Mao proclaimed the establishment of the People's Republic of China. He then announced the formation of a new communist style government, and called for local party organizations to select delegates to attend the first Chinese People's Political Consultative Conference in September, 1949, at which laws and institutions would be established to maintain the revolution. The following selection is a portion of his speech to the opening session of this congress, in which he outlined his concept of China's past, present, and future.

OPENING SPEECH AT THE FIRST PARTY CONGRESS, SEPTEMBER 21, 1949

Our conference is composed of more than six hundred delegates, representing all the democratic parties and organizations of China, the People's Liberation Army, the various regions and localities, and the nationalities all over China as well as the overseas Chinese. This shows that ours is a conference of great unity of the people of the whole country.

The achievement of this great unity among the people throughout the entire country has been made possible by our defeat of the reactionary Kuomintang government, which was aided by American imperialism. In a period of just over three years, the heroic Chinese People's Liberation Army,.... crushed the offensive of the several million troops of the U.S.-aided Kuomintang reactionary government and turned to launching its own counter-offensive.... In just over three years' time, the people all over the country have united together to aid the People's Liberation Army and oppose their enemy, and they have won basic victory. It is on this foundation the current People's Political Consultative Conference is convened....

Within a period of just over three years, the Chinese people, led by the Communist Party of China, have quickly awakened and organized themselves into a nationwide united front to fight against imperialism, feudalism, bureaucratic capitalism, and the Kuomintang reactionary government, which represents these things in a concentrated form. They aided the People's War of Liberation, basically struck down the Kuomintang reactionary government, and toppled the rule of imperialism in China....

Fellow delegates, we all share the feeling that our work will be written down in the history of humanity; it will show that the Chinese people, forming one quarter of humanity, have now stood up. The Chinese have always been a great, courageous, and industrious nation, and it is only in modern times that they have fallen behind. This falling behind came entirely as a result of the oppression and exploitation by foreign imperialism and domestic reactionary governments. For over a century our forebearers have never stopped waging tenacious struggles against domestic and foreign oppressors, including the Revolution of 1911 led by Mr. Sun Yat-sen, the great forerunner of the Chinese revolution. Our forebearers have instructed us to fulfill their behest, and we have now done so accordingly. We have united and have overthrown both domestic and foreign oppressors through the People's War of Liberation and the people's great revolution, and now proclaim the establishment of the People's Republic of China. From now on our nation will join the great family of peace and freedom loving nations of the world. We will work with courage and diligence to create our own civilization and well-being, and at the same time promote world peace and freedom. Our nation will never again be a nation insulted by others. We have stood up. Our revolution has won the sympathy and acclamation of the broad masses of the people throughout the world. Our friends are all over the world....

Our state system of the people's democratic dictatorship is a powerful weapon for safeguarding the fruits of the victory of the people's revolution and for thwarting the foreign and domestic enemies in their plots to stage a comeback. We must firmly grasp this weapon. Internationally, we must unite with all countries and peoples who cherish peace and freedom, first of all with the Soviet Union and the various New Democracies, so that we will not become isolated in our struggle to safeguard the fruits of the victory of the people's revolution.... So long as we uphold the people's democratic dictatorship and unite with international friends, we shall forever be victorious....

Following the advent of an upsurge in economic reconstruction, there will inevitably appear an upsurge of cultural reconstruction. The era in which the Chinese people were regarded as uncivilized is now over. We will emerge in the world as a highly civilized nation.

Our national defense will be consolidated, and no imperialist will be allowed to invade our territory again. Our people's armed forces must be preserved and developed with the heroic and tested People's Liberation Army as the foundation. We will not only have a powerful army but also a powerful air force and a powerful navy.

Let the domestic and foreign reactionaries tremble before us!.... Eternal glory to the people's heroes who have given their lives to the People's War of Liberation and to the People's Revolution! Hail to the victory of the People's War and People's Revolution!

TEXTUAL QUESTIONS FOR ANALYSIS

1. Who does Mao blame for the relative decline of China? What does he mean when he says that the Chinese people have "stood up?"
2. Obviously his use of terms does not mean the same as those used by Western political

leaders of the 1940's and 1950's. What does he mean by the apparently contradictory term "people's democratic dictatorship?" How does he view the role of the American government in China's recent history?
3. Based on your text, what parts of his future program did come into existence?
4. Based on this selection and your text, explain why, in spite of costly failures in his policies, Mao is still highly regarded in China today.

Source: Mao Tse-tung, "Opening Speech at the First Plenary Session of the CPPCC," *Daily Bulletin 634* (October 2, 1952), (New China News Agency), pp. 3-4,5.

CHAPTER 54
AFRICA AFTER INDEPENDENCE

South Africa gained independence from Great Britain in 1910, and established a legal system of racial segregation based on white rule. But the whites of South Africa were themselves divided in their political views, with most of those of English descent favoring a low-key approach to racial discrimination, and the Boers, the descendants of the original Dutch settlers of the seventeenth and eighteenth centuries, favoring a much stricter and more blatant form of white control of the black majority. In 1948 the predominantly Boer National party gained control of South Africa's government for the first time, and quickly adopted the policy of "apartheid," a term meaning "apartness" in Afrikaans, the Dutch dialect of the Boers. Under this system of laws, all South Africans were to be racially classified as either Bantu (all black Africans), Colored (those of mixed race), Asian (Indian or Pakistani), and White. Within a few years the government had established separate residential areas in cities for each group, forbade marriage and most social contact between each group, restricted separate jobs for each group, prohibited non-white voting and office holding, and forced all blacks to live in so-called "homelands."

The primary black group fighting against racism in South Africa was the African National Congress, founded in 1913. The original primary goal of the ANC was to foster unity among the numerous African tribes and ethnic groups of South Africa; their methods consisted mainly of petitions and direct appeals for concessions to white political leaders. After the adoption of apartheid, the ANC sponsored non-violent campaigns of passive resistance and gave support to strikes of black labor unions. These campaigns led the government to adopt a more openly violent campaign of repression, and this in turn led some black leaders to call for the use of force against the government.

Nelson Mandela, an active ANC organizer and lawyer since the 1940's, was one of those young black leaders who became frustrated by the government's use of force against peaceful protest and its unwillingness to consider any modification in apartheid. After the government outlawed the ANC in 1960, he went underground, and helped establish a group that carried out bombings in several South African cities. Arrested in 1964, he was convicted of treason, and was imprisoned until 1990 when the National party prime minister F.W. de Klerk ordered his release. De Klerk had become convinced that apartheid had to go if South Africa was to survive economically or politically, and in 1991 he sponsored the repeal of the most important apartheid laws. Over the next three years the rest of the system was dismantled, and in the new multi-racial South Africa Mandela was elected President in 1994 and began the process of attempting to gain the support of all South Africans in the effort to rebuild the nation.

The following selection is part of Nelson Mandela's opening statement defending his actions at his trial in 1964 before an all-white court. Here he defends his support of a campaign of sabotage and attempts to give the court some idea of the plight of black South Africans.

NELSON MANDELA'S SPEECH TO THE COURT, APRIL 20, 1964

In my youth.... I listened to the elders of my tribe telling stories of the old days. Amongst the tales they related to me were those of wars fought by our ancestors in defense of the fatherland.... I hoped then that life might offer me the opportunity to serve my people and make my own humble contribution to their freedom struggle. This is what has motivated me in all that I have done in relation to the charges made against me in this case....

I have already mentioned that I was one of the persons who helped to form Umkonto ("Spear of the Nation-" the sabotage group Mandela formed). I, and the others who started the organization, did so for two reasons. Firstly, we believed that as a result of Government policy, violence by the African people had become inevitable, and unless responsible leadership was given to canalize and control the feelings of our people, there would be outbreaks of terrorism which would produce an intensity of bitterness and hostility between the various races of this country which is not produced even by war. Secondly, we felt that without violence there would be no way open to the African people to succeed in their struggle against the principles of White supremacy. All lawful modes of expressing opposition to this principle had been closed by legislation, and we were placed in a position in which we had either to accept a permanent state of inferiority, or to defy the Government.

But the violence which we chose to adopt was not terrorism. We who formed Umkonto were all members of the African National Congress, and had behind us the ANC tradition of non-violence and negotiation as a means of solving political disputes. We believed that South Africa belonged to all the people who lived in it, and not to one group, be it Black or White. We did not want an interracial war, and tried to avoid it to the last minute....

The African National Congress was formed in 1912 to defend the rights of the African people.... For thirty-seven years- that is until 1949- it adhered strictly to a constitutional struggle. It put forward demands and resolutions; it sent delegations to the Government in the belief that African grievances could be settled through peaceful discussion and that Africans could advance gradually to full political rights. But White Governments remained unmoved, and the rights of the Africans became less instead of becoming greater....

Even after 1949, the ANC remained determined to avoid violence. At this time, however, there was a change from strictly constitutional means of protest which had been employed in the past. The change was embodied in a decision which was taken to protest against apartheid legislation by peaceful, but unlawful, demonstrations against certain laws. Pursuant to this policy the ANC launched the Defiance Campaign, in which I was placed in charge of volunteers. This campaign was based on the principles of passive resistance. More than

8,500 people defied apartheid laws and went to jail. Yet there was not a single instance of violence in the course of this campaign on the part of any defier....

In 1960 there was the shooting in Sharpeville (police killed 69 and wounded 178 anti-apartheid demonstrators), which resulted in the proclamation of a state of emergency and the declaration of the ANC as an unlawful organization. My colleagues and I, after careful consideration, decided that we would not obey this decree. The African people were not part of the Government and did not make the laws by which they were governed....

Four forms of violence were possible. There is sabotage, there is guerrilla warfare, there is terrorism, and there is open revolution. We chose to adopt the first method and exhaust it before taking any other decision.

In the light of our political background the choice was a logical one. Sabotage did not involve loss of life, and it offered the best hope for future race relations. Bitterness would be kept to a minimum and, if the policy bore fruit, democratic government could become a reality....

It is true that there has often been close cooperation between the ANC and the Communist Party. But cooperation is merely proof of a common goal- in this case the removal of White supremacy- and is not proof of a complete community of interests....

It is perhaps difficult for White South Africans, with an ingrained prejudice against communism, to understand why experienced African politicians so readily accept communists as their friends. But to us the reason is obvious. Theoretical differences amongst those fighting against oppression is a luxury we cannot afford at this stage. What is more, for many decades communists were the only political group in South Africa who were prepared to eat with us, talk with us, live with us, and work with us. They were the only political group which was prepared to work with Africans for the attainment of political rights and a stake in society. Because of this, there are many Africans who, today, tend to equate freedom with communism....

Our fight is against real, and not imaginary, hardships.... Basically, we fight against two features which are the hallmarks of African life in South Africa and which are entrenched by legislation which we seek to have repealed. These features are poverty and lack of human dignity, and we do not need communists or so-called "agitators" to teach us about these things.

South Africa is the richest country in Africa, and could be one of the richest countries in the world. But it is a land of extremes and remarkable contrasts. The Whites enjoy what may well be the highest standard of living in the world, whilst Africans live in poverty and misery.... There are two ways to break out of poverty. The first is by formal education, and the second is by the worker acquiring a greater skill at his work and thus higher wages. As far as Africans are concerned, both these avenues of advancement are deliberately curtailed by legislation....

The lack of human dignity experienced by Africans is the direct result of the policy of White supremacy. White supremacy implies Black inferiority. Legislation designed to preserve White supremacy entrenches this notion....

During my lifetime I have dedicated myself to this struggle of the African people. I have fought against White domination, and I have fought against Black domination. I have cherished the ideal of a democratic and free society in which all persons live together in harmony and with equal opportunities. It is an ideal which I hope to live for and to achieve. But if needs be, it is an ideal for which I am prepared to die.

TEXTUAL QUESTIONS FOR ANALYSIS

1. What were the early stages of ANC protest against apartheid? Why did Mandela and other leaders finally decide to adopt direct and violent opposition?
2. What forms of direct action were open to them, and which did they decide upon and why? Might there have been other reasons that he did not state? What might they be?
3. What were the worst features of apartheid according to Mandela? Why was communist support welcomed by ANC leaders?
4. Why would a Boer political leader have found Mandela's remarks threatening?

Source: Nelson Mandela, *No Easy Walk to Freedom* (New York: Basic Books, 1965), pp. 163-168, 180-181.

CHAPTER 55
LATIN AMERICA IN THE TWENTIETH CENTURY

Cuba became an American protectorate under the terms of the treaty that gave it independence at the end of the Spanish-American War in 1898. American interference in Cuban affairs thus began in the late nineteenth century and continued up until the 1960's. United States policy was to support a variety of strong pro-American leaders, and encourage investment in the island. Democratic reforms were not considered essential, or necessarily desirable. In the 1940's a Cuban soldier named Fulgencio Batista staged a coup and established himself in power in Havanna. He was ousted in 1944 and spent the next five years in exile in the United States. In 1952, he was returned to power by the army and established a military dictatorship friendly to the United States.

A group of young revolutionaries, led by a young law student named Fidel Castro, formed an organized group dedicated to Batista's overthrow and calling for the establishment of a constitutional state independent of American influence and without military control. Castro was arrested in 1953 and spent two years in prison, and then another two years in exile. In 1956 he launched the "26th of July Movement" and began a guerrilla war in the mountains of Cuba designed to bring down the Batista government. He attempted to portray himself as a Cuban patriot and a genuine disciple of democracy, struggling against overwhelming odds. In reality the Batista regime was corrupt and its armed forces undisciplined, and when it became clear the United States would not intervene to save the military dictator, he fled in 1959 to comfortable retirement and exile in the Dominican Republic.

Castro attempted to influence American opinion throughout his career as a guerrilla leader. He allowed American news reporters to travel with his troops and invited young Americans to volunteer in his army. In 1957, *Coronet Magazine,* a popular American weekly, gave him the opportunity to write a short article defining his real goals, and the following selection is taken from that article that appeared in the February, 1958 issue. When Castro wrote this article he was still a bearded young revolutionary looking for support wherever he could find it, so undoubtedly a good deal of what he said, especially in light of his later actions, was what he thought Americans wanted to hear. He needed the good will of America if he was to succeed in his military campaign, and he certainly hoped to undercut American support for the Batista regime. Shortly after coming to power, he held public trials and public executions of former Batista officials, seized the property of American businesses, revealed himself to be a Marxist, and set up a one party Communist dictatorship in Cuba. Cuba's alliance with Russia and American opposition to Cuba's exportation of Communist influence would be central features of the Cold War from 1960 to the collapse of the Soviet Union in 1991, but all of that was in the future when the young Castro wrote the following article for an American public that knew little about him.

WHY WE FIGHT, FIDEL CASTRO, FEBRUARY 1958

As this is written, our armed campaign on Cuban soil against Cuba's dictatorial regime is entering its second year. Though it has been given many meanings and many interpretations, it is essentially a political struggle. In this struggle, we have sustained a few reverses and a good many victories, while dictator Batista can point to a single successful achievement: he has effectively muzzled all public communications in our country, silenced TV, radio, and the press, and so intimidated our news publishers that not a single Cuban reporter has ever been assigned to *our* side of what is, in effect, a spreading civil war.

.... In obtaining and publishing this exclusive article- the only first-person story written by me since we landed in Cuba on December 2, 1956- *Coronet Magazine* has given us the opportunity to state our aims and to correct the many errors and distortions circulating about our revolutionary struggle.

Though dictatorship, ignorance, military rule, and police oppression have spawned a great many evils among our people, all these evils have a common root: the lack of liberty. The single word most expressive of our aim and spirit is simply- freedom. First of all and most of all, we are fighting to do away with dictatorship in Cuba and to establish the foundations of genuine representative government.

To attain this, we intend to eject from office Fulgencio Batista and all his cabinet officers; to place them under arrest and impeach them before special revolutionary tribunals. To replace the unconstitutional Batista regime, we will aid in setting up a provisional government to be nominated by a special convention made up of delegates of our various civic organizations: Lions, Rotarians, professional bodies such as the physicians' or engineers' guilds, religious associations, and so forth. This will be a break with established procedure, but we feel certain that it will prove workable. Once appointed, the provisional government's chief task will be to prepare and conduct truly honest general elections within twelve months.

The question has presented itself whether I aspire to the presidential office of this provisional government or the elected government which will succeed it. The truth is that, quite apart from my personal reluctance to enter the presidential competition so soon, our Constitution, as it now stands, would prohibit it. Under its age requirement clause, I am, at 31, far too young to be eligible for the presidency, and will remain so for another ten years.

We do have, however, a number of program points which might serve as a basis for action by the provisional government. They are the following:

1. Immediate freedom for all political prisoners, civil as well as military....
2. Full and untrammeled freedom of public information for all communication media- broadcasting, TV, the daily and periodical press. Arbitrary censorship and systematic corruption of journalists has long been one of the festering sores of our nation.
3. We want to reestablish for all citizens the personal and political rights set forth in our much-ignored Constitution.
4. We want to wipe out corruption in Cuban public life. Those who have grown accustomed over the years to dealing with venal policemen, thieving tax collectors, and rapacious army bosses here in Cuba may think this an optimistic resolution. But we intend to attack this problem at its very roots, by creating a career civil service beyond the reach of politics and nepotism and by making sure that our career functionaries get paid enough to be able to live without having to accept bribes.
5. We want to sponsor an intensive campaign against illiteracy....
6. We are in favor of land reform bills adjusting the uncertain owner-tenant relations that are a peculiar blight of rural Cuba. Hundreds of thousands of small farmers occupy parcels of land which they do not own under the law. Thousands of absentee owners claim title to properties they have hardly ever seen.... We will support no land reform bill, however, which does not provide for the just compensation of expropriated owners.
7. Finally, we support speedy industrialization of our national economy and the raising of employment levels.

Apart from the political misconceptions about my ambitions and those of our movement- we have often been accused of plotting to replace military dictatorship with revolutionary dictatorship- nothing has been so frequently misunderstood as our economic program. Various influential U.S. publications have identified me as a tool of big business, as a dangerous radical, and as a narrow reactionary manipulated by the clergy. U.S. companies with business interests in Cuba have been repeatedly warned that I have secret plans in my pocket for seizing all foreign holdings.

Let me say for the record that we have no plans for the expropriation or nationalization of foreign investments here.... I personally have come to feel that nationalization is, at best, a cumbersome instrument. It does not seem to make the state any stronger, yet it enfeebles private enterprise. Even more importantly, any attempt at wholesale nationalization would obviously hamper the principal point of our economic platform- industrialization at the fastest possible rate. For this purpose, foreign investments will always be welcome and secure here.

Industrialization is at the heart of our economic progress. Something must be done about the staggering mass of over one million unemployed.... A million unemployed in a nation of six million bespeaks a terrible economic sickness which must be cured without delay, lest it fester and become a breeding ground for communism....

And with rising living standards and growing confidence in government will come rapid progress toward political stability under a representative, truly democratic government. That, ultimately, is what we are fighting for....

TEXTUAL QUESTIONS FOR ANALYSIS

1. How many statements did Castro later prove to be false?
2. Why would this article have appealed to most Americans in 1958? Do you think Castro was attempting at least in part to say what he thought Americans wanted to hear?
3. How many parts of his program did he carry out? How many did he either ignore or forget?
4. Although he said he had no presidential ambitions and that he was too young to serve, Castro has served as the leader of Cuba since 1959. How do you think he would explain this statement and this article today?

Source: Fidel Castro, "Why We Fight," *Coronet, February 1958* (New York: Esquire Inc., 1958).

CHAPTER 56
THE REEMERGENCE OF THE MUSLIM WORLD

No one individual is more closely identified with the Islamic revival of the post-World War II era than Ayatollah Ruhullah Khomeini. Following in the steps of his grandfather and father he became a religious scholar, and by the 1930's was the head of a prestigious Islamic school in the pilgrimage city of Qum in Iran. By the late 1960's he had become one of the most vocal and prestigious critics of the Shah's regime. He publicly and repeatedly denounced the Shah's pro-U.S. policies, his dictatorial rule, and his efforts to minimize the role of Islam in Iranian society. In 1963 widespread rioting broke out directed against the policies of the Shah, and inspired by the teachings of religious scholars like Khomeini. He was arrested and sent into exile, where he continued to denounce the Shah and his policies. Exile took him to Turkey, Iraq, and France, before his triumphant return in 1979.

The following selection is an excellent example of the type of appeal Khomeini used during his time in exile, and provides some answers as to why Islamic fundamentalists blamed the United States and the West in general for the problems of the Middle East. Rioting had broken out in the city of Qum once again in January, 1978, caused by articles in the official government controlled press insulting Khomeini. The government sent in troops and dozens of demonstrators were killed, wounded, or arrested. Khomeini delivered this speech from exile in Iraq in February, 1978, and it was later printed and distributed secretly in Iran to commemorate the sacrifices of those who dared to oppose the Shah's regime. By January 1979 the Shah had fled Iran, and in February 1979, almost exactly a year after this speech, Khomeini returned from exile to proclaim the Islamic Republic of Iran.

IN COMMEMORATION OF THE FIRST MARTYRS OF THE REVOLUTION

All the miseries that we have suffered, still suffer, and are about to suffer soon are caused by the heads of those countries that have signed the Declaration of Human Rights (Universal Declaration of Human Rights adopted by the United Nations in 1948), but that at all times have denied man his freedom. Freedom of the individual is the most important part of the Declaration of Human Rights. Individual human beings must all be equal before the law, and they must be free. They must be free in their choice of residence and occupation. But we see the Iranian nation, together with many others, suffering at the hands of those states that have signed and ratified the Declaration.

The U. S. is one of the signatories to this document. It has agreed that the rights of man must be protected and that man must be free. But see what crimes America has committed against man. As long as I can remember- and I can remember back further than many of you, for you are younger than I- America has created disasters for mankind. It has appointed its agents in both Muslim and non-Muslim countries to deprive everyone who lives under their domination of his freedom. The imperialists proclaim that man is free only in order to deceive the masses. But people can no longer be deceived. All these declarations they make, supposedly in favor of human rights, have no reality; they are designed to deceive.... What we have said is true not only of America but also of Britain, another power that signed and ratified the Declaration of Human Rights- Britain, whose civilization and democracy everybody praises so much without realizing that they are repeating the propaganda slogans Britain is cunningly feeding people; Britain, which is meant to practice true constitutionalism! But have we not see, despite all this propaganda, what crimes Britain has committed in India, Pakistan, and its other colonies?

The imperialist states, like America and Britain, brought Israel into existence, and we have seen what misery they have inflicted on the Muslim peoples by means of Israel, and what crimes they are now committing against the Muslims....

As for America, a signatory to the Declaration of Human Rights, it imposed this Shah upon us, a worthy successor to his father. During the period he has ruled, this creature has transformed Iran into an official colony of the U.S. What crimes he has committed in service to his masters!

What crimes that father and son have committed against the Iranian nation since their appointment by the signatories to the Declaration of Human Rights. All they have to offer humanity is repression; we have witnessed part of it, and we have heard part of it....

The Iranian government granted absolute immunity to the American advisers and got a few dollars in exchange. How many American officers there are in Iran now, and what huge salaries they receive! That is our problem- everything in our treasury has to be emptied into the pockets of America, and if there is any slight remainder, it has to go to the Shah and his gang. They buy themselves villas abroad and stuff their bank accounts with the people's money, while the nation subsists in poverty....

What happens to all that money? Is our country poor? Our country has an ocean of oil. It has iron; it has precious metals. Iran is a rich country. But those so-called friends of humanity have appointed their agent to rule this country in order to prevent the poor from benefiting from its riches. Everything must go into his masters' pockets and be spent on their enjoyment....

The imperialists know full well how active the religious scholars are, and what an activist and militant religion Islam is. So they drew up a plan to bring the religious scholars into disrepute, and for several centuries propagated the notion that religion must be separated from politics. Some came to believe it and began asking, "What business do we have with politics?" The posing of this question means the abandonment of Islam; it means burying Islam in our religious schools....

May God Almighty grant all of you success. May God Almighty remove this evil from rule over the Muslims. May God, Exalted and Almighty, preserve our people in the midst of their tribulation. May God, Exalted and Almighty, grant the Muslims a favorable result in this, their struggle.

And peace be upon you, and the mercy and blessings of God.

TEXTUAL QUESTIONS FOR ANALYSIS

1. According to Khomeini, what is wrong with Iran and who is responsible?
2. How does he characterize the Westernizing policy of the Shah?
3. What is the solution to the problems of Iran? Does he believe that there should be a separation of church and state, as is the practice in the West?
4. Based on what you have read in your text, how successful was Khomeini in solving the problems of Iran? What changes indicated in the above speech did he bring about?

Source: H. Algar, trans., *Islam and Revolution* (Berkeley, California: Mizan Press, 1981), pp. 275-277.

CHAPTER 57
THE MARXIST COLLAPSE

The collapse of the Soviet Union in 1991 was one of the pivotal events of the post-World War II era. The Cold War between the United States and the USSR had dominated world politics for over four decades and had brought the world to the brink of nuclear war on several occasions. In one of the great ironies of twentieth century history, it was not a brutal totalitarian dictator that helped to bring about the demise of Soviet style communism, but a well educated, and reform-minded career politician, Mikhail Gorbachev. In 1985, he was only fifty-four when he was picked by the Politburo to become the leader of the Soviet

Union. A true believer in Marxism, he felt that the problems that plagued the USSR stemmed from the corruption of the original principles of communism, not from the contradictions inherent in the system itself. He announced soon after assuming power the twin policies of perestroika (restructuring) and glasnost (openness) that he believed would provide the means for the revival of true communism. He was most known in the West for his sincere desire to ease tensions and negotiate arms reductions with the United States, a policy that soon produced results in a series of treaties with Presidents Reagan and Bush. In 1987 he became the first Soviet leader since Lenin to write a book, PERESTROIKA, in which he outlined his views of the problems facing the USSR and how his policies would result in a revived, productive, peaceful, and incorruptible Marxist society. With a clear appreciation of the importance of the good will of the Western powers, the book was published in Europe and the United States, as well as Russia. The following selection is from that book, and provides clear insight into the views of this ardent communist reformer.

PERESTROIKA

Russia, where a great Revolution took place seventy years ago, is an ancient country with a unique history filled with searchings, accomplishments, and tragic events. It has given the world many discoveries and outstanding personalities.

However, the Soviet Union is a young state without analogues in history or in the modern world. Over the past seven decades- a short span in the history of human civilization- our country has traveled a path equal to centuries. One of the mightiest powers in the world rose up to replace the(backward semi-colonial and semi-feudal Russian Empire....

At some stage- this became particularly clear in the latter half of the seventies- something happened that was at first sight inexplicable. The country began to lose momentum. Economic failures became more frequent. Difficulties began to accumulate and deteriorate, and unresolved problems to multiply. Elements of what we call stagnation and other phenomena alien to socialism began to appear in the life of society....

Analyzing the situation, we first discovered a slowing economic growth. In the last fifteen years the national income growth rates had declined by more than a half and by the beginning of the eighties had fallen to a level close to economic stagnation. A country that was once quickly closing on the world's advanced nations began to lose one position after another....

The presentation of a "problem-free" reality backfired: a breach had formed between word and deed, which bred public passivity and disbelief in the slogans being proclaimed. It was only natural that this situation resulted in a credibility gap: everything that was proclaimed from the rostrums and printed in newspapers and textbooks was put in question. Decay began in public morals; the great feeling of solidarity with each other that was forged during the heroic times of the Revolution, the first five-year plans, the Great Patriotic War (World War II), and postwar rehabilitation was weakening; alcoholism, drug addiction, and crime were growing; and the penetration of the stereotypes of mass culture alien to us, which bred vulgarity and low tastes and brought about ideological barrenness increased....

An unbiased and honest approach led us to the only logical conclusion that the country was verging on crisis. This conclusion was announced at the April 1985 Plenary Meeting of the Central Committee (the policy making body of the USSR), which inaugurated the new strategy of perestroika and formulated its basic principles....

Today our main job is to lift the individual spiritually, respecting his inner world and giving him moral strength. We are seeking to make the whole intellectual potential of society and all the potentialities of culture work to mold a socially active person, spiritually rich, just, and conscientious. An individual must know and feel that his contribution is needed, that his dignity is not being infringed upon, that he is being treated with trust and respect. When an individual sees all this, he is capable of accomplishing much.

Of course, perestroika somehow affects everybody; it jolts many out of their customary state of calm and satisfaction at the existing way of life. Here I think it is appropriate to draw your attention to one specific feature of socialism. I have in mind the high degree of social protection in our society. On the one hand, it is, doubtless, a benefit and a major achievement of ours. On the other, it makes some people spongers.

There is virtually no unemployment. The state has assumed concern for ensuring employment. Even a person dismissed for laziness or a breach of labor discipline must be given another job. Also, wage-leveling has become a regular feature of our everyday life: even if a person is a bad worker, he gets enough to live fairly comfortably.... We have enormous sums of money concentrated in the social funds from which people receive financial assistance.... Health care is free, and so is education. People are protected from the vicissitudes of life, and we are proud of this.

But we also see that dishonest people try to exploit these advantages of socialism; they know only their rights, but they do not want to know their duties: they work poorly, shirk, and drink hard. There are quite a few people who have adapted the existing laws and practices to their own selfish interests. They give little to society, but nevertheless managed to get from it all that is possible and what even seems impossible; they have lived on unearned incomes.

The policy of restructuring puts everything in its place. We are fully restoring the principle of socialism. "From each according to his ability, to each according to his work," and we seek to affirm social justice for all, equal rights for all, one law for all, one kind of discipline for all, and high responsibilities for each. Perestroika raises the level of social responsibility and expectation....

Perestroika means mass initiative. It is the comprehensive development of democracy, socialist self-government, encouragement of initiative and creative endeavor, improved order and discipline, more glasnost, criticism, and self-criticism in all spheres of our society. It is utmost respect for the individual and consideration for personal dignity.

Perestroika is the all-round intensification of the Soviet economy, the revival and development of the principles of democratic centralism in running the national economy, the universal introduction of economic methods, the renunciation of management by injunction and by administrative methods, and the overall encouragement of innovation and socialist enterprise....

The essence of perestroika lies in the fact that *it unites socialism with democracy* and revives the Leninist concept of socialist construction both in theory and practice. Such is the essence of perestroika, which accounts for its genuine revolutionary spirit and its all embracing scope.

The goal is worth the effort. And we are sure that our effort will be a worthy contribution to humanity's social progress.

TEXTUAL QUESTIONS FOR ANALYSIS

1. According to Gorbachev, what are the major problems facing the Soviet Union? How long have these problems been evident?
2. Gorbachev defends central planning in running the national economy, but says that perestroika calls for more initiative and creativity from the workers. What is the contradiction here?
3. Summarize what you think Gorbachev means by perestroika. Do you think such a concept could be implemented and maintain the socialist system?
4. In Gorbachev's view, what will perestroika mean to the average worker in Soviet society?

Source: Mikhail Gorbachov, *Perestroika* (New York: Harper Collins, 1987), pp. 18, 19, 30-32.

CHAPTER 58
AT THE END OF THE TWENTIETH CENTURY

Final chapters of world history texts are difficult to write, for they deal with the future, which historians are reluctant to predict. Trends that appear to be irreversible may be reversed; disasters that appear unavoidable, may be avoided. But with all of these unpredictable questions, there is still value in making informed assessments of the present in order to guide future decisions. One of the institutions that makes a business of assessing the present in order to make recommendations about the future is the United Nations. The following selection is a summary of a UN report on the differences in development between the various nations of the world and recommendations to alleviate these differences. It appeared on May 16, 1993, in the *Los Angeles Times,* and provides a good overview of the state of the world at the end of the twentieth century.

UNITED NATIONS REPORT ON HUMAN DEVELOPMENT

Despite sweeping political, economic, and social changes around the world, fewer than 10% of people worldwide now participate fully in the institutions and decisions that shape their lives, according to a new report from the United Nations.

Disparities among ethnic, gender, and economic groups are stark, even in the United States, which now ranks sixth after Japan, Canada, Norway, Switzerland, and Sweden on the Human

Development Index that rates standards of living.

But when ranked by ethnic groups, U.S. whites rank first in the world, while African Americans come in 31st, after poor Caribbean nations like Trinidad and Tobago.

Latino Americans come in 35th, after struggling former Soviet satellites like Estonia.... and just ahead of Chile, Russia, and Malta....

Yet the report cites the United States not for its inequities but for its successes and the implications for the rest of the world.

"The United States has a commendable record on human rights and affirmative action. It is an open society, with nondiscrimination written into law and a media that keeps pressure on the issue.... But the United States still has grave problems, which only shows how far most other countries have to go."

Almost every country has at least one and often several underprivileged ethnic groups whose education, political access, economic opportunities, and life expectancy fall seriously below the national average, the report says.

The infant mortality rate among Guatamala's Indians is 20% higher than that of the rest of the population. In South Africa, half the population, mostly whites, own 88% of all private property.

More than a billion of the world's people- or one in every five- still languish in absolute poverty, for example, while the poorest fifth find that the richest fifth enjoy more than 150 times their income....

The gap between rich and poor is widening in several countries. Between 1970 and 1988, real income of the richest 20% of Chile's population grew by 10%, while income of the poorest 20% fell by 3%.

Participation in a country's economic life has also been blocked by the new trend in "jobless growth." Between 1960 and 1987, the economies in Germany, France, and Britain more than doubled, yet their employment rate dropped....

The case of women offers another stark example. Although they form a majority globally, women are vastly underrepresented in political systems, occupying only about 10% of parliamentary seats and fewer than 4% of Cabinet posts, the UN report says....

The UN report also outlines five major steps to reconstruct societies and expand participation- what it calls "five new pillars of a people-centered world order." They are:
1. Shift the focus of security from nations to people, from armament to development....
2. Develop new patterns of national and global governing and decentralize power, giving more authority to local governments....
3. Focus new international cooperation on human needs rather than on the preference

of states....
4. Reorient markets to serve people rather than people serving markets....
5. Develop and invest in new models of development that people-centered and sustainable environmentally....

Overall, the report concedes that its recommendations "call for nothing less than a revolution in our thinking."

TEXTUAL QUESTIONS FOR ANALYSIS

1. What are some of the most obvious and serious disparities that exist today?
2. Are these disparities dangerous to world peace and why or why not?
3. What would be required to implement the first two recommendations of the UN report?
4. Would these recommendations really require a "revolution in our thinking?" Why or why not?

Source: *Los Angeles Times,* May 16, 1993, pp. 2-3.